INSIDE THE EARTH
Evidence from Earthquakes

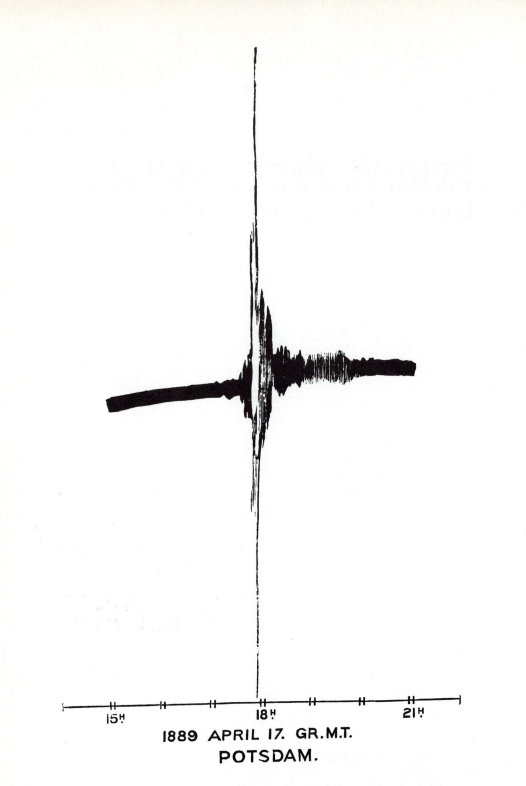

1889 APRIL 17. GR.M.T.
POTSDAM.

The first recognized recording of ground shaking from an earthquake source
on the other side of the world (Japan).

INSIDE THE EARTH
Evidence from Earthquakes

Bruce A. Bolt
University of California, Berkeley

W. H. FREEMAN AND COMPANY
San Francisco

Project Editor: Patricia Brewer
Designer: Sharon Helen Smith
Production Coordinator: Bill Murdock
Illustration Coordinator: Richard Quiñones
Artist: Eric Hieber
Compositor: Graphic Typesetting Service
Printer and Binder: The Maple-Vail Book Manufacturing Group

Library of Congress Cataloging in Publication Data

Bolt, Bruce A., 1930-
  Inside the earth.

  Bibliography: p.
  Includes index.
  1. Earth—Interior.   2. Seismology.   I. Title.
QE509.B69   551.1′1   81-17431
ISBN 0-7167-1359-4   AACR2
ISBN 0-7167-1360-8 (pbk.)

Printed in the United States of America

1 2 3 4 5 6 7 8 9 0   MP   0 8 9 8 7 6 5 4 3 2

To the memory of
Richard Dixon Oldham (1858–1936)
and to the other pioneers

Contents

Preface

This book is for all those—students and nonspecialists—who are curious about the physical properties inside our planet Earth. In writing it, I have been able to incorporate some of my interests in geophysics over the last twenty years. This pleasure has been heightened by the opportunity to illustrate the ideas more than is usual in science books. Simplified diagrams do shed light where words alone often fail.

Much of the discussion is based on elementary measurements of earthquake waves, recorded by instruments called seismographs. Without a guide, most people, even trained scientists, see these earthquake recordings as wiggly lines without form or meaning, and there have been few written attempts to explain how the wiggles carry news about the deep interior of the Earth. At the same time, the story of our search for the structure inside the Earth enables us to highlight the peculiar nature of geophysical work. In most sciences, the objects of study are measured directly, but direct observations of the rocks deeper than a few tens of kilometers are quite impossible. This account is thus one for those who enjoy detective stories in the Sherlock Holmes tradition. If a criminal is seen committing a crime, there is no mystery. If from a multitude of clues—some second-hand and some circumstantial—we must weigh the evidence and cross-check our inferences, then the case grips our imagination. This is the situation when we probe inside the Earth with earthquake waves. What I have done is summarize the main clues gleaned from earthquake studies.

More than most sciences, seismology—the study of earthquakes and related effects—is international. Since the first earthquake observatories were established around 1900, it has been clear that earthquake measurements from individual observatories have to be pooled in order to be sensibly interpreted. A single earthquake observatory, working in splendid isolation, can make only a limited contribution to the resolution of the constitution of the Earth. Knowledge of the deep parts of the globe has drawn on readings from seismographs located on all continents and has involved scientists from many countries. Growth of this knowledge continues to depend on such cooperation and exchange of earthquake data.

The student must not expect, in this introductory treatment, to find complete coverage of studies of the Earth's structure and physical composition. Though the contents of the book cover a major part of the subject of seismology, every chapter could be substantially expanded. It is hoped, however, that the text does give a clear explanation of a central part of geophysics to undergraduates in physics and the earth sciences and to others interested in more than a casual summary of present knowledge of the interior of our planet.

My introduction to the subject extends back to 1958 when K. E. Bullen, Professor of Applied Mathematics at the University of Sydney, set me the problem of examining the observational basis for a strange transition shell that, it had been suggested, might surround the inner core of the Earth. Ever since, exploration of the heart of the Earth has fascinated me. Because of the surge in this work, particularly in the last decade, this slim volume must contain only a selection from the published results. Naturally enough, controversies and differences of opinion concerning the details of structure and physical properties have arisen. I had space to present only a few of the most gripping arguments, and I apologize that the color of other major investigations has been omitted.

Although references to individual contributions have not been made in the text, I have included, in the Guide to Further Reading, suggestions that cover most of the basic developments up to 1981. Many recent important ideas and arguments are available only in research articles in specialized journals. Neither have I tried to compile references on the history of the subject, but the reader who is interested in early writings can consult the account of S. G. Bush and the citations listed in the classical books by Harold Jeffreys, Beno Gutenberg, and K. E. Bullen. The text itself is free of mathematics, but some elementary and commonly used mathematics is given in boxes. Chapter 8 is composed of problems, some of which involve a little algebra and calculus.

I owe a debt to many colleagues and students who have worked with me on aspects of the material. In particular, I wish to thank R. D. Adams, R. A. Hansen, J. A. Jacobs, O. Nuttli, C. Sonett, J. Stifler, and R. Uhrhammer for helping iron out faults and providing information. C. H. Chapman generously made available a computer program that calculates and plots families of seismic rays in the

Earth's interior; many of the fine ray diagrams were drawn using his program. D. Michniuk and P. Murtha also computed ray diagrams and helped in other ways. I wish to express my thanks to my wife Beverly, who read the proof sheets and made valuable comments and suggestions. Also, my thanks are due to R. Miller and R. McKenzie for great assistance in preparing figures, to N. Abrahamson for work on the exercises, and to A. McClure for ably typing much of the text.

The writing was completed in spring 1980 at Cambridge, England, while I was on a Churchill Overseas Fellowship, and I am most grateful to the Master and Fellows at Churchill College and to the Department of Geodesy and Geophysics for the warmest hospitality.

November 1981   Bruce A. Bolt

INSIDE THE EARTH
Evidence from Earthquakes

Richard Dixon Oldham (1858–1936)
"*Geologists have turned in despair from the
[constitution of the Earth] leaving its center as a
playground for mathematicians.*"

CHAPTER 1

Evolution
of Knowledge
# of Middle Earth

The Pre-seismological Age

The first three figures of this chapter illustrate the spectacular progression of knowledge of the interior structure of our planet. In ancient times, myth and legend pictured the center of the Earth as an "underworld" of mystery, heat, and violence (Figure 1.1). There, Dante toured in quiet horror through the dark passageways. During Greek times, speculations on the underground world were much affected by volcanoes erupting in the Aegean and Mediterranean. Descriptions were given of vast subterranean caverns in which hot sulfurous winds and gases blew fiercely, often causing violent quaking of the ground. The Bible speaks of the fiery furnace of Hades.

With the growth of modern science after Isaac Newton, a more mechanical outlook developed, which drew analogies between the unknown interior and the properties of surface rocks. The theory of gravity had a critical effect on speculations on the inside of the Earth. As a direct consequence of Newton's ideas on gravitational attractions between massive bodies, astronomer Nevil Maskelyne in 1774–1776 used a simple but brilliant scheme to weigh the whole Earth. By means of the deflection of a plumb line by the mountain Schiehallion in Scotland (see Box 1.1) he determined the mean density of the Earth to be 4.5 g/cm^3, i.e., 4.5 times that of water and twice that of granite. A little later in 1798, Lord Cavendish improved this estimate using a torsion rod and two leaden balls as attracting masses to determine the constant of gravitation (G), and hence (from equation

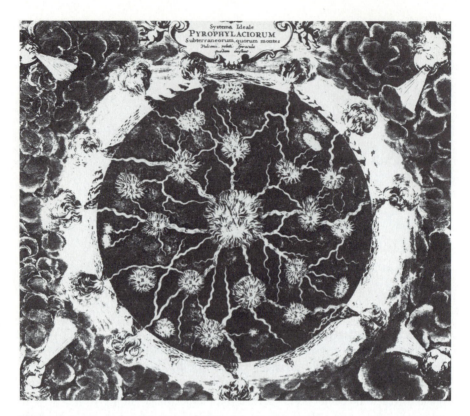

Figure 1.1   An early view (about 1800) of the Earth's interior. The writer conceived of Earth as a ball of solid material fissured by tubes of magma, connecting pockets of eruptive gases to volcanic vents on the Earth's surface.

(3) in Box 1.1) a mean density of the Earth of 5.45 g/cm^3, close to the modern value of 5.52. Even by the beginning of the nineteenth century, therefore, it was known that the average density of the Earth as a whole was about double that of common rocks. The odds were thus very high that there are not only no great cavities at profound depths in the Earth but also that the material there must be very dense.

By the mid-nineteenth century, measurements of arcs of the meridian at various places on the Earth's surface had shown that the shape of the Earth is really ellipsoidal and not exactly a sphere. The equatorial radius is 20 km longer than the polar radius. Mathematicians of the time took as a primitive assumption that the Earth acquired this ellipsoidal shape when it was once entirely liquid. They speculated that the liquid globe had been deformed by a combination of the

Box 1.1 Weighing the Earth

Newton's famous law for the force of attraction between two masses m and M, distance R apart, is

$$F = \frac{GmM}{R^2} \qquad (1)$$

The factor G is Newton's constant of gravitation and must be estimated by a difficult experiment. Nevil Maskelyne was able to measure the mass of the Earth M_E by using equation (1) without first knowing G. Then, because he knew the radius of the Earth R_E, he could calculate the Earth's average density ($=$ mass/volume).

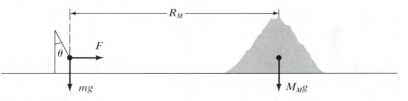

Let m be the mass of a small metal plumb bob suspended a distance R_M from the mountain, mass M_M. Then the force F pulling the plumb bob toward the mountain, when the acceleration of gravity is g, is

$$F = mg \tan \theta = \frac{GmM_M}{R_M^2} \qquad \text{[from (1)]} \qquad (2)$$

But the weight of the bob due to the Earth's pull downward is

$$mg = \frac{GmM_E}{R_E^2} \qquad \text{[from (1)]} \qquad (3)$$

Thus, equating mg from (2) and (3):

$$M_E = \frac{R_E^2}{R_M^2} \cdot \frac{M_M}{\tan \theta} \qquad (4)$$

All terms on the right-hand side have measured values.

mutual gravitation of its parts and the centrifugal forces due to the spin of the Earth. It is then a small step to believe that the Earth's ellipticity depends on the way that rocks of different density are distributed with depth in the Earth. They then made other plausible assumptions, for instance, that the increase of density toward the center of the Earth might be caused by heavier material sinking, or perhaps it was due to the gigantic central pressures. If the *whole* of the increase of density toward the Earth's center was caused by compression, then the rate of change of density with depth could be worked out.

In the latter case, there were four known qualities: the density of surface rocks, the Earth's average density, the effect of pressure on density, and the effect of density on ellipticity. Nineteenth century mathematicians were able to connect these quantities by equations. With the known density of surface rocks as a start (say 2.5 g/cm^3), solutions of these equations enabled the variation of density from the surface to the center of the Earth to be calculated. There was always the proviso that the mean density obtained should agree with that measured by Cavendish. Such ingenious but simple arguments led to estimates of density at the center of the Earth of 10 to 12 g/cm^3. According to present estimates (Chapter 7), these early values were close to the bull's-eye.

After finding numerical values for the mean density and central density of the Earth, the next step was to compare them with densities of known minerals, compounds, and elements. For example, 12 g/cm^3 is four and one-half times the density of quartz and one and one-half that of iron at ordinary pressure and temperature, but it is not much higher than the density of silver at surface conditions and lower than that of gold. (Not until the early twentieth century could the prize of a huge volume of gold residing at the center of the planet be ruled out!)

Another important subject of speculation last century was the temperature inside the Earth. It was known from mining operations that the temperature of the rocks increases with increasing depths. In deep mines, this gradual increase of temperature becomes serious, rendering labor a great trial. Already by 1870, actual measurements of the rate of temperature increase with depth had been made by lowering thermometers in holes in the rock in deep mines and in artesian boreholes. The average rate of increase was about one degree Celsius for 30 meters of descent. The snag is that if this rate of increase continues even deeper the temperature of the interior would become enormous; at only a depth of 500 kilometers, for example, it would exceed 10,000°C. The inference is that the high rate of temperature increase measured at the surface does not continue uniformly to great depths or we would arrive at temperatures exceeding that

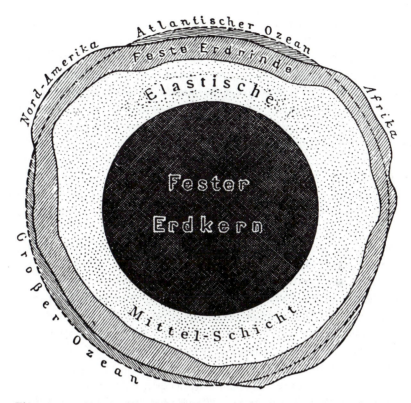

Figure 1.2   Sketch of the Earth's interior published in Berlin in 1902
(H. Kraemer). The Earth has three shells: a solid crust (Feste Erdrinde)
supported by an elastic mantle (Elastische Mittel-Schicht) wrapped around a
solid central core (Fester Erdkern). The change from Figure 1.1 reflects
an improved physical understanding, but the model is still limited by
lack of seismological data.

thought to occur at the surface of the Sun. A reasonable alternative, in the view
of the early geophysicists, was that the Earth was cooling inward from the surface
and outward from the center. The concept thus emerged of a mainly solid Earth
containing a spherical nucleus (see Figure 1.2) that was perhaps liquid or liquid
and viscous gas.* This nucleus was surrounded by a solid rocky shell which was

*In 1793, Benjamin Franklin surmised that because gases are more compressible than metals, they
could furnish the high densities presumed for the central regions.

layered, and from geological field evidence, perhaps differed in density and thickness in different localities of the world.

Other clues to the deep interior came, of course, from measurements of the heat brought to the surface by magma and gases in volcanic eruptions. Sir Humphry Davy ascribed volcanic heat to the oxidation of material in the deep interior of the Earth. An alternative idea was put forward by the engineer Robert Mallet, who was one of the founders of seismology. He believed that the heat of volcanic action was derived from the work of crushing rocks beneath the surface. Because he knew that steel, for example, contracts when it cools, he thought that the crushing was due to the contraction of the interior of the Earth through its cooling over a very long time. This idea of contraction of the Earth as a driving force for the formation of mountains and ocean troughs survived as a hypothesis and, until about 1970, was perhaps the majority view held by geologists and geophysicists.

The discovery of radioactivity in 1896 by the French physicist Henri Becquerel delivered a sudden shock to the arguments. The seemingly inexorable contraction of the Earth because of cooling required major rethinking because it was determined that all rocks in their natural state contain small amounts of radioactive elements. The radioactive decay of these elements continually gives off additional heat and thus tends to counteract the cooling of an originally molten Earth by radiation into space. (Indeed, the planet may now be heating up from radioactive heating.)

The natural philosophers of the pre-seismological era pondered yet another clue to the state inside the Earth. The attraction exerted by the Sun and Moon on the Earth raises tides in the oceans. If the Earth were not exceedingly rigid but more or less liquid, the surface of the Earth itself would rise and fall just like the tides of the oceans (see Figure 6.1). At any seacoast the tidal movements would occur together, and ocean tides would not be seen. Sir William Thomson (later Lord Kelvin) remarked, "the solid crust would yield so freely to the deforming influence of the sun and moon that it would simply carry the waters of the ocean up and down with it, and there would be no tidal rise and fall of water relative to land."

From this idea, it is only a small mathematical step to estimate the average rigidity of the Earth's interior using heights and phases of observed ocean tides at the principal ports. By 1887, George Darwin (second son of Charles Darwin) had concluded from the study of tides that the "geological hypothesis of a fluid interior is untenable," and that the overall rigidity of the Earth's interior is considerable although not as great as that of steel. Later we will give the modern estimates for the rigidity of the deep interior (Chapter 7), and we will see that Darwin was only partly correct.

Before leaving this rapid review of the pre-seismological era it is well to make sure that the reader is aware of the very broad brush used in the early geophysical work. Such arguments just cannot resolve detailed variations in interior properties. Indeed, there was room for many wide differences of opinion, and no final victories were won in the battles between those who believed the interior was largely fluid (liquids and gases) and those who, like George Darwin, thought of it as largely solid.

Figure 1.2 illustrates only one speculative model of Earth widely accepted at the end of the nineteenth century. The physical and mathematical arguments on density and temperature gave a picture of a slightly flattened planet with a solid crust (possibly quite thick) floating on an elastic or, in some models, a plastic substratum. In this description there was a solid nucleus.

The models with partially liquid or plastic interiors naturally led to speculation that there was very slow circulation of the viscous rock, like convection currents set up in a pot of boiling oil. Because buoyancy would keep the lighter rocks whether liquid or solid, toward the surface, the silicate rock in the crust was thought to be on the average less dense than the rock (probably rich in iron) in the substratum, in general agreement with the considerations of density discussed previously. These speculations were reinforced by observations of lava lakes at Vesuvius and Kilauea where a crust would often solidify on the top of viscous molten lava.

This concept of slow churning of vast convection cells in the upper part of the Earth was to fall into disfavor in the first half of the twentieth century but was adopted readily for the nucleus. Even more recently, very slow convection of plastic rock in the upper substratum has again been widely considered. These swings in belief on internal motions occurred for reasons that go beyond the scope of this book. The reader is referred to the papers in *Earthquakes and Volcanoes* for an introductory discussion (see the Guide to Further Reading).

The Seismological Age

At the turn of this century there was a crucial break in the hitherto unresolvable debate on the architecture of the Earth's interior—the onset of the seismological age. In medicine, X-rays are passed through the human body, and a photographic plate reveals a pattern of black and white tones that an experienced eye can interpret in terms of body structure. In much the same way, when an earthquake occurs, its waves travel through the body of the Earth and are recorded by seismographs at earthquake observatories. These seismic waves carry with them to the surface information on the structure through which they have passed. The basic question is how to decipher the recorded waves and so, in effect, X-ray our planet. As with X-ray plates, the seismograms from earthquakes show the silhouette of the Earth's structure as "through a glass, darkly," and much experience and analysis must be applied in order to obtain a clearer focus.

The first decisive steps were based on simple enough principles. In Japan in 1883, the English seismologist John Milne surmised that "it is not unlikely that every large earthquake might with proper appliances be recorded at any point of the globe." This prediction was fulfilled in 1889 when E. von Rebeur Paschwitz "was struck by the coincidence in time" between the arrival of singular waves, registered by delicate horizontal pendulums at Potsdam and Wilhemshaven in Germany, and the time of the great earthquake in Tokyo at $2^h 7^m$ on April 18 (see frontispiece). He concluded that "the disturbances noticed in Germany were really due to the earthquake in Tokyo." The new era had begun.

In 1897, such seismograms from distant earthquakes were shown by R. D. Oldham of the Geological Survey of India to consist of three separate disturbances or wave types that followed each other in succession (as on frontispiece). They were called at that time the first and second (usually small) "preliminary tremors" and the "large waves." With this separation in mind Milne plotted, for a number of earthquakes, the time of transit of both the preliminary tremors and large waves against the distance they had traveled between wave source and recording seismograph. He suggested, moreover, that the distance to the source or origin point could be approximately determined by measuring the interval of time by which the large waves were outraced by the preliminary tremors. If this interval is known for three or more stations, then the location of the origin can be spotted by drawing arcs on a globe. The systematic application of the technique by Milne and others led to the rapid compilation of the first truly global catalogs of earthquake centers and world seismicity maps. (This ingenious method of earthquake source location by remote observatories is still used.)

Oldham then quickly established (in 1900) that the "preliminary tremors," called primary (P) and secondary (S) waves, traveled through the interior of the Earth while the large waves propagated close to the surface of the Earth. The stage was thus set for the first seismological triumph on the Earth's deep structure. In a paper that is a delight to read even today (see Box 1.2), Oldham supplied in 1906 (the year of the great San Francisco earthquake) the first "X-ray" evidence that the Earth has a large distinct central core.

Oldham's discovery was made by a straightforward argument, and although excusably wrong in some specifics, is essentially still used today to establish the existence of a deep-seated discontinuity. First, we should note that in seismology it is convenient to measure distances on the surface of the Earth, not as the number of kilometers along the curved surface, but as the angle in degrees subtended at the Earth's center. Thus, a recording station at the anticenter of an earthquake is 180° distant from the earthquake source.

To give an idea of the way Oldham reached his hypothesis, let us consider a large hypothetical earthquake centered at the South Pole. From such an earthquake, seismologists observe that the preliminary P waves are recorded rather uniformly throughout the southern hemisphere and up to about 15° north of the equator, i.e., up to the latitude of Guatemala, a distance of 105° or so. What is more, the transit times of these waves fall along a smooth curve when plotted against angular distance. Seismograms from observatories at more northerly latitudes like California indicate that a significant change from uniformity has occurred. The actual curve and data points published by Oldham are reproduced in Box 1.2. In the graph in Box 1.2, Oldham had only a few points at great distances, but those beyond 130° lie about 2 minutes later than the trend of the points for smaller distances and it is not possible to draw a smooth curve through them all.

Such a delay would mean that the P waves had begun to travel through a region where their speed was much less. But Oldham concentrated on the "second phases" (i.e., the S waves). He pointed to the remarkable delay at 130° of 10 minutes for the second phases. Oldham explained this delay by the hypothesis that these S waves have penetrated a central core that transmits seismic S waves at a distinctly slower rate (about half) than the surrounding shell. Immediately he went on to estimate also the size of the core by assuming that the wave paths are straight lines or chords. (Actually, as we will see, they are concave outward in most of the interior (see Figure 1.3).)

Oldham's argument, which can be followed easily from the ray diagram in Box 1.2, was that "the core is not penetrated by wave paths which emerge at 120°, and the great decrease at 150° shows that the wave paths emerging at this distance have penetrated deeply into it. Because the chord at 120° reaches a maximum depth from the surface of half the radius, it may be taken that the central core does not extend beyond about 0.4 of the radius R from the center." Incidentally, Oldham explicitly rejected the supposition that S waves were extinguished by the central core, but contrary to the logic given in many modern textbooks, still allowed that the core might be fluid. (The present view is that the delayed second phases shown in Box 1.2 beyond 130° are actually reflected S waves (called SS—see Chapter 2), traveling entirely in the mantle.) In Chapter 4 we will give a modern explanation of the curves of the first tremors given in Box 1.2.

The first quantitative estimate of $0.4R$ or 2550 km for the radius of the core was much improved in 1914 when Beno Gutenberg, working in Germany with

Box 1.2   The Seismological Discovery
of the Earth's Core

The Constitution of the Interior of the Earth, as Revealed by Earthquakes. By Richard Dixon Oldham, F.G.S. (Read February 21, 1906)

I. Introductory.

Of all regions of the earth none invites speculation more than that which lies beneath our feet, and in none is speculation more dangerous; yet, apart from speculation, it is little that we can say regarding the constitution of the interior of the earth. We know, with sufficient accuracy for most purposes, its size and shape; we know that its mean density is about 5½ times that of water, that the density must increase towards the centre, and that the temperature must be high, but beyond these facts little can be said to be known. Many theories of the earth have been propounded at different times: the central substance of the earth has been supposed to be fiery, fluid, solid, and gaseous in turn, till geologists have turned in despair from the subject, and become inclined to confine their attention to the outermost crust of the earth, leaving its centre as a playground for mathematicians.

The object of this paper is not to introduce another speculation, but to point out that the subject is, at least partly, removed from the realm of speculation into that of knowledge by the instrument of research which the modern seismograph has placed in our hands. Just as the spectroscope opened up a new astronomy by enabling the astronomer to determine some of the constituents of which distant stars are composed, so the seismograph, recording the unfelt motion of distant earthquakes, enables us to see into the earth and determine its nature with as great a certainty, up to a certain point, as if we could drive a tunnel through it and take samples of the matter passed through. The subject is yet in its infancy, and much may ultimately be expected of it; already some interesting and unexpected results have come out, which I propose to deal with in this paper.

From R. D. Oldham, "The Constitution of the Interior of the Earth, as Revealed by Earthquakes," *Quarterly Journal, Geological Society, 62,* 456–475, 1906.

more extensive seismological travel times, gave the depth to the core boundary as 2900 km, or a radius of about $0.545R$. This value has stood the test of time, and present estimates are within a few kilometers of Gutenberg's value (see Chapter 4).

After Oldham's work, it became more and more clear to observational seismologists, from studying the P and S preliminary tremors, that beyond about 105° there was a shadow zone in which the preliminary waves from distant earthquakes were absent or very weak. Thus, in the hypothetical earthquake discussed above centered at the South Pole, seismographs in Mexico and the United States would not, or only weakly, detect the P waves, but beyond about 142°, in Canada and

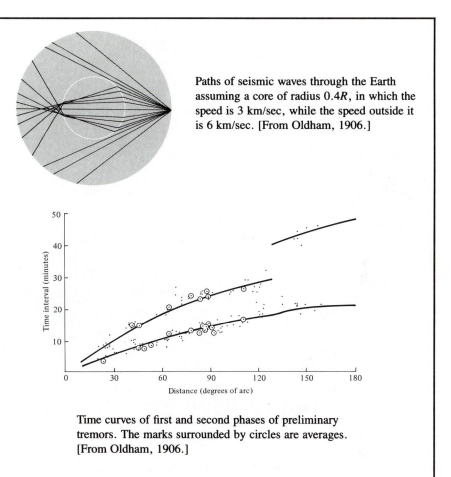

Paths of seismic waves through the Earth assuming a core of radius $0.4R$, in which the speed is 3 km/sec, while the speed outside it is 6 km/sec. [From Oldham, 1906.]

Time curves of first and second phases of preliminary tremors. The marks surrounded by circles are averages. [From Oldham, 1906.]

Alaska, they would again come in rather strongly but be delayed by several minutes. In other words, the great central core casts a shadow in the form of a dark band around the surface of the Earth between distances of about 105° and 142°. Such screening behavior was, in fact, predicted by Oldham's hypothesis of a central nucleus of different elastic properties, since seismic waves entering the core would suffer considerable refraction similar to refraction of light through a spherical lens (see Box 1.2 and Figure 4.7).

It was also learned during these exciting early days of discovery that the second preliminary tremor or S wave traveled like P waves through all parts of the Earth's outer shell or mantle (except the oceans and limited pockets of molten rock).

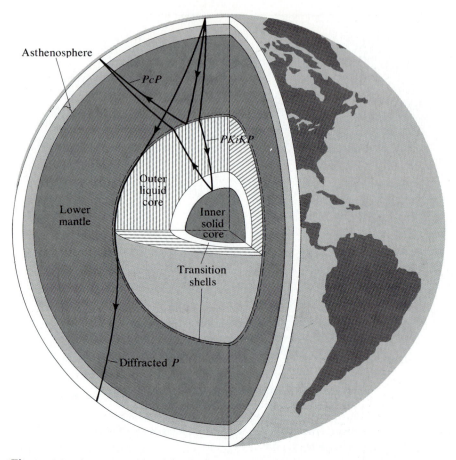

Figure 1.3   A cross section of the Earth based on the most recent seismological evidence. The outer shell consists of a rocky mantle that has structural discontinuities in its upper part and at its lower boundary that are capable of reflecting or modifying earthquake waves. Below the mantle an outer fluid core surrounds a solid kernel at the Earth's center; between the two is a transition shell. The paths taken by three major kinds of earthquake waves are shown. The waves reflected from the outer liquid core are designated *PcP;* the waves reflected from the inner solid core are *PKiKP;* and the waves that creep around the liquid core are diffracted *P*. [From Bruce A. Bolt, "The Fine Structure of the Earth's Interior." Copyright © 1973 by Scientific American, Inc. All rights reserved.]

Because it was known that the *S* wave disturbance involved distortional shearing of the rocks (a deformation that would occur in elastic solids but not in liquids) the recognition of both *P* and *S* waves to distances of about 105° was regarded as a strong argument in favor of the solidity of the outer part of the Earth.

This situation was different for the central core. Recordings of earthquakes at great distances not only indicated weaknesses in wave energy and a large time delay in the first preliminary tremor (*P* waves), but it was not clear that the second preliminary tremor (*S* waves) was being recorded at all by the seismographs.

Also, in the first decade of the century, another fundamental discovery was made concerning the Earth's outermost shell or crust. In 1909, Andrija Mohorovičić at the Zagreb (Yugoslavia) Seismographic Observatory found the first convincing evidence for a sharp boundary separating the crustal rocks from rock in the shell below (now called the mantle). He followed a method similar to that used by Oldham for great distances, and plotted on a graph, for relatively short or regional distances, a curve of observed time of travel against distance for *P* waves from Balkan earthquakes. Mohorovičić found a sharp bend near a distance of 200 km (an angular distance of about two degrees) and explained the bend by supposing that at a depth of 50 km there was an abrupt change in the properties of the rock. A great deal of later work by other seismologists showed this change to be worldwide but located at various depths (see Chapter 4). The boundary separates what is now conventionally called the *crust* from the mantle below, and it has come to be called the Mohorovičić discontinuity or *Moho*, for short.

Before we leave this review of the dawn of the seismological era, it is hard to resist giving a round of applause for the brilliant and profound work done in a very short time by the early seismologists. From the recognition by von Rebeur Paschwitz of the Japanese earthquake on records in Europe half a world away, only 25 years elapsed before Oldham (1906), Mohorovičić (1909), and Gutenberg (1914) located the core and crust. These years must have been for the few workers in seismology at the time a most exhilarating era. Now we can only share their delight in retrospect by reading their papers. Oldham and Milne did their early work, of course, before Nobel Prizes and other valuable awards were instituted. Milne died in 1913 and Oldham* lived on until 1936, but neither has received wide recognition in the history of science. It seems strange that no Nobel Prizes in physics (instituted in 1901) are awarded even today for discoveries of structure within our planet but are for those within the minute world of the atom.

Direct and Inverse Problems

Exploration of the inner Earth is at once fascinating and frustrating. Indeed, what confidence can we ever have about statements made on the properties of the deep

---

*H. Jeffreys remarked that the geologist R. D. Oldham was the only scientific pioneer he had known who showed little interest in his own (seismological) discoveries.

interior? Because these properties are not directly measured, results are of a different kind from the determination of, say, the height of a mountain or the temperature of a geyser. Before we embark on descriptions of the Earth's interior, therefore, we need first to outline the difficulties we will meet along the road and to determine how far we can go in committing ourselves to conclusions about underground structure. The skeptical reader should see not only how geophysical problems differ from familiar ones in the accessible world, but also how qualitative estimates can be made.

In this book, the limelight is given to measurements of the transit times, amplitudes, and frequency content of earthquake waves. These waves pass through the Earth from their source (usually fault rupture) and are recorded by seismographs on the Earth's surface. Of course, such seismic wave measurements are not the only geophysical data used in probing the Earth, but they underpin the whole enterprise.

During this century, irresistible economic forces have stimulated the use of geophysical techniques of all kinds as strenuous efforts have been made to discover mineral and energy resources from ore bodies, geothermal and oil and gas fields. Although these specialized exploration methods generally lie outside the scope of this book, the exploration of deep planetary structure has many parallels in mineral exploration. Certainly in the oil industry, in particular, techniques using seismic waves for discovering structures likely to contain gas or oil have been brought to a high level of sophistication. A petroleum exploration company carries out specially designed field measurements of seismic waves, produced on the surface by explosives or mechanical shakers. Measurements of the recorded waves are processed using computer programs to detect and locate anomalous zones in the uppermost layers of the crust. On these inferences, expensive decisions on drilling programs must be based, and in this economically competitive mill geophysical methods are tested and ultimately checked by deep boreholes.

When we go more deeply inside the Earth, however, beyond the reach of surface borings (say, below 10 km), many of the successful seismological methods in exploration for minerals in the upper few kilometers of the Earth become less practical. Because the dimensions of deep underground structures range from hundreds to thousands of kilometers, the number of seismographs spread over a region or continent that are required to maintain the same resolution as in oil prospecting becomes prohibitively expensive. Also, because oceans cover three-quarters of the surface, seismographs have not in the past been able to operate with the necessary uniform geographical distribution on the Earth's surface. (Nowadays, watertight seismograph systems have been designed to operate for moderately long times on the floor of deep oceans.) The most decisive difference, however, is that the artificial sources of wave energy used in mineral exploration are not nearly energetic enough to produce signals that will penetrate to profound depths with enough strength to be detected at distant places. The exceptions are the massive underground nuclear explosions that produce wave energy comparable to moderate earthquakes, and, as we will see later, seismic waves from them have been clearly detected at distant observatories.

Let us now consider the kind of information that we need to find structures deep in the Earth. Such structures would be, for example, sharp boundaries that separate rock types of different physical (and perhaps chemical) properties, such as liquid and solid states. We might fancy to ask: are the main structural boundaries within the Earth of global extent or are they mainly local in scale? That is, does the Earth's interior look like an onion with layers that are symmetric about the Earth's center, or does it look like a Christmas pudding with localized masses or rocks of different types and states scattered throughout?

Help with such queries comes by considering analogies with other situations that are known to us directly. Indeed, argument by analogy is of fundamental importance in probing deep regions, and in this book many analogies will be drawn to help explain physical behavior not often experienced in everyday life. Of course, with argument by analogy there is some danger that we may be misled, but if carefully chosen, such comparisons not only help us to see through the subterranean mists but also suggest further exploration.

To take an example from modern-day navigation, echo-sounders on ships, using reflection of sound waves from the sea floor, help mariners chart the depth to the ocean bottom and so navigate safely. Such methods require only that the speed of sound in sea water be known. By analogy, we may be able to use an energetic source of seismic waves, such as a large earthquake, and measure on seismographs the time it takes for the waves to reflect down and back to the Earth's surface from sharp boundaries at depth. Indeed, such reflection methods are one of the most powerful ways in which earthquakes can be used to study the architecture of the Earth's interior. We immediately, however, hit a snag. Unlike the speed of sound waves in water, the speed of earthquake waves in the rocks of the Earth's interior is not known initially. Thus, if the reflection method is to be used not only to detect but also to locate deep structure, the velocity of waves in rocks as a function of depth must first or simultaneously be determined. How can this be done?

It is helpful to look at the problem slightly differently. Suppose that we know the speed of earthquake waves throughout the Earth. Then, by dividing the transit distance by the speed, it is easy enough to calculate the time that the waves take to go from an earthquake source to a seismograph at any given place on the

Earth's surface. In other words, we could predict when the earthquake waves would arrive at the observatory. This type of problem is said to be "direct." That is, if the properties of the inaccessible interior were known, direct calculation would predict when the waves would be observed on the Earth's surface. The actual situation is, roughly speaking, the opposite. We have measurements of the travel times of earthquake waves at a finite number of places on the Earth's surface, and from these we must determine both the speed of waves in the rocks and the structural changes within the Earth (see Box 1.3).

The latter type of problem occurs in many parts of science and everyday experience, and is called an "inverse problem." We can give a simple illustration. Suppose we ski down the mountain trail in Figure 1.4. We want to measure the undulations of the ski slope from the top to the valley floor. Now, if we knew the topography of the slope, we could calculate easily enough (ignoring snow and wind resistance) the time it would take to ski from the top to the valley floor. This is the direct problem. Instead, not knowing the shape of the slope, we start skiing at a number of points on the slope, and we use a stopwatch to clock the time of travel at the finish line in each run. After making many runs, the plot of run times against each starting position might look like the graph in Figure 1.4. It is obvious that the shape of this graph contains in it the information that we seek in order to answer the inverse problem, that is, what is the shape of the ski slope? Various ways to answer such questions, at least approximately, have been devised. It could be done, for example, just by trial and error; many slopes could

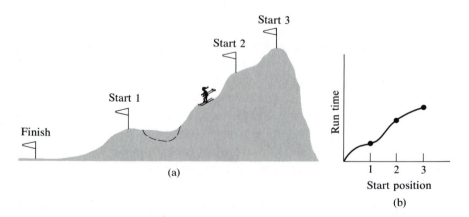

Figure 1.4   (a) A ski run with various starting points. (b) A graph of the ski time from the start to the finish as a function of the starting position. A small change in topography (indicated by the dashed line on the mountain slope) results in a small change in the curve of time against position.

Box 1.3 Connection Between Travel Times and Velocities

Plots of travel times T of seismic rays against angular epicentral distance Δ (delta) degrees provide the basic observational function

$$T = f(\Delta) \tag{1}$$

The point A defines the ray that travels to a distance Δ_1 in time T_1. At A, let the slope of the tangent $dT/d\Delta$ be p_1.

The problem is to transform from the travel-time–distance diagram to the plot of seismic velocity v against the radius in the form

$$v = F(r) \tag{2}$$

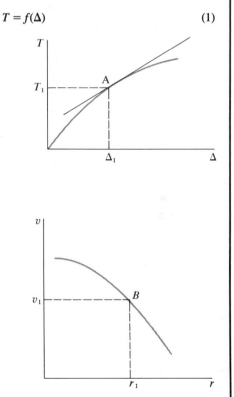

The point B defines the depth $r_0 - r_1$ in the Earth of radius r_0 at which the velocity is v_1 and the ray at point A bottoms.

The essential transformation between (1) and (2) was derived by Herglotz (1907) and Bateman (1910).

The gradients of (1) are used from Snell's law (See Box 2.1) in the form

$$P_1 = \frac{r_1}{v_1} \tag{3}$$

Then

$$\pi \log\left(\frac{r_0}{r_1}\right) = \int_0^{\Delta_1} \cosh^{-1}\left(\frac{p}{p_1}\right) d\Delta \tag{4}$$

Because p is known as a function of Δ from (1), unless there are complications in the T, Δ curve, the integration can be carried out for a family of rays between $\Delta = 0$ and $\Delta = \Delta_1$. Then, we have r_1 as a function of p_1, and thus from (3), v_1 as a function of r_1.

be tried until one is found that gives a close fit between the calculated times and those observed on the stopwatch.

Immediately, there is an intriguing twist. In the ski problem, it would be found that many slopes give travel times that agree with the observed points. Basically this is because the mountain slope is made up of an infinite number of points so no matter how often we ski the slope, we can never provide enough points to define the continuous slope with all its moguls and bumps. This non-uniqueness is typical of inverse problems and it certainly occurs in probing the Earth's deep interior. Fortunately, most people are satisfied with the common sense view that we are not generally interested in every tiny undulation of the slope but only the major ones. In other words, the answer is good enough if we assume that the slope is more or less smooth, with undulations that are longer than our skis, for example. This limit on the information required enables us to match the number of bumps on the slope with the finite number of ski runs that are made.

The conclusion from this analogy is that experimental results about the inaccessible parts of the Earth will have certain basic limits in *resolution*. Interestingly, this aspect of resolution is not a consequence of the care with which the measurements themselves can be made (i.e., the accuracy of reading the stopwatch or measuring the length of the run). The measurements, indeed, may be very accurate, yet, because the measurements are limited in number, we are free, within limits, to adopt a variety of solutions. Errors of reading introduce yet other types of imprecisions into the answers of any inverse problem and must, of course, be taken into account.

In summary, when we try to infer hidden properties of the deep interior from surface measurements, we are always faced with the problem of non-uniqueness of our conclusions. We are forced to abstract the main structural features from the almost endless complexity of Earth structure and in so doing the estimates we obtain are blurred in resolution by the limited number of measurements and blurred in precision by the errors in the measurements themselves. A warning is appropriate here. Nowadays, with fast computers with large memories, some current studies are being made using tens and even hundreds of thousands of measurements of seismic waves. While precision can be improved this way, the answers can never be exact for a single point in the deep interior. We will always have to be content with average and smoothed values, yet as we will see, such information is often robust and sufficient for the purposes at hand.

It is appropriate to round off this discussion of the indirect way knowledge is gained about the deep parts of the Earth by considering briefly the discovery of the inner core.

In following up R. D. Oldham's work seismologists observed that the first preliminary tremors (P waves) that had passed through both the mantle and the core—then denoted by P' but nowadays called *PKP* waves—could, in very favorable circumstances, be seen on seismograms at distances less than the bounding distance of 142°. This weak illumination within the shadow of the massive central core was attributed to diffraction of seismic waves, just as light diffracts around a sharp object (see p. 171).

At the Copenhagen Seismological Observatory, the young Danish seismologist Inge Lehmann had for a number of years been clearly observing waves through the core from Pacific earthquakes. She felt that core waves could be classified into three separate types, which she denoted P'_1, P'_2, and P'_3. The standard explanation for the first two of these waves as drawn in Box 1.4 was that the rays were defracted at the boundary between the mantle and core and focused toward the antipodes (in Box 1.4, P'_1 is ray 3 and P'_2 is ray 2a). After much thought, she rejected the diffraction interpretation for P'_3 and explained the P'_3 waves as reflections from another sharp discontinuity within the core itself (in Box 1.4, P'_3 is ray 5).

Inge Lehmann had attended the first coeducational school in Denmark, which was founded and maintained by Hanna Adler, an aunt of Niels Bohr. In an autobiographical note, she recalled that boys and girls were treated completely alike in the school. "No difference between the intellect of boys and girls was recognized, a fact that brought me disappointments later in life when I had to realize that this was not the general attitude." She graduated from the University of Copenhagen in mathematics and physical science and began her work in seismology in 1925. In 1928, she was appointed Chief of the Seismological Department of the Royal Danish Geodetic Institute, a post she held until her retirement in 1953. By 1936, she had already 10 years' experience with interpretation of seismograms and a knowledge of the scientific method needed to make a decisive step forward.

Let us consider how Lehmann drew the key inference and thus discovered the inner core. Her first step was to calculate a direct problem. She assumed an Earth model that was particularly simple. It had constant velocities in the mantle (10 km/sec) and core (8 km/sec). These were reasonable average values for both regions. She then introduced a small central core which again had a constant velocity. These simplifications enabled her to take the seismic rays to be straight lines (chords), and so travel times could be calculated by elementary trigonometry. She then showed by successive adjustments that a reasonable velocity and radius of the inner core could be found that predicted a travel-time curve close to the observations of the travel times of the P'_3 waves. In effect, she proved an existence theorem: a plausible three-shell Earth structure could be defined that explained the features of the observed waves.

She argued that the current hypothesis of diffraction was not satisfactory to

Box 1.4 The Seismological Discovery of the Earth's Inner Core

$$P'$$

By I. Lehmann

An explanation of the P'_3 wave is required, since now it can hardly be considered probable that it is due to diffraction. A hypothesis will here be suggested which seems to hold some probability, although it cannot be proved from the data at hand.

We take it that, as before, the earth consists of a core and a mantle, but that inside the core there is an inner core in which the velocity is larger than in the outer one. The radius of the inner core is taken to be $r_1 = \dfrac{8}{10} r_0 \sin 16° = 0.2205 \, r_0$, so that the ray whose angle of incidence at the surface of the earth is 16° just touches the inner core.

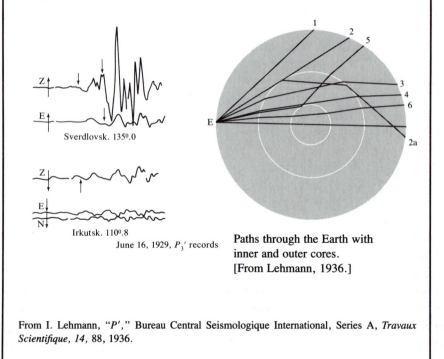

Sverdlovsk. 135°.0

Irkutsk. 110°.8

June 16, 1929, $P_3{}'$ records

Paths through the Earth with inner and outer cores.
[From Lehmann, 1936.]

From I. Lehmann, "P'," Bureau Central Seismologique International, Series A, *Travaux Scientifique, 14,* 88, 1936.

explain the core *P* waves far from the bounding or focal point (e.g., at Irkusk at 110.8° in Box 1.4). She demonstrated in a simple way that *P* waves reflected from the inner core could emerge at distances between 105° and 142° as indicated in path 5.

Inge Lehmann's discovery of the inner core was thus more complicated than is generally understood by the discovery of, say, a distant land or of a new comet. Her work, however, did convince Beno Gutenberg in the United States and Harold Jeffreys in England that her hypothesis of the inner core was a viable one. Within two years they had independently carried out more detailed calculations involving many observed travel times of *P'* waves and calculated by an inverse method both the radius of the inner core and the *P*-velocity distribution in it. In summary, the discovery of the last major discontinuity within our globe was a mixture of direct and inverse procedures. Lehmann was careful (see the quotation in Box 1.4) to state in her paper (with one of the shortest titles in seismology) that she had not *proved* the existence of an inner core. Indeed, in the strict sense, certain proof of deep structure can never be obtained by earthquake probes.

Complementary Worlds of Time and Frequency

We can picture the inside of the Earth within two frameworks or windows. These windows complement each other; each provides insights that are not easily perceived from the other. We will characterize these windows as "the domain of time" and "the domain of frequency." From childhood, the time domain is familiar to us by the passage of the days and the passing of objects. When we perceive waves on water or waves across a field of wheat, it is normal to see them passing a certain place in a certain interval of time. In this respect, the seismograms that illustrate this book (e.g., Figure 3.4) are splendid examples of seeing waves through a time window. The seismograms picture the wavy motion of the ground as the earthquake passes by. In the time domain we can fix the time of arrival of various waves such as Milne and Oldham did with the preliminary tremors, watch the wave patterns wax and wane, and measure the total duration of the motion. In this type of perception, we are able to enjoy the evolving wave patterns and think of them in terms of different amplitudes and frequencies that change as time goes on.

Alternatively, let us look for a moment through a less familiar window into the frequency domain. Here we see a different view of wave properties. At first, the perception is strange, like Alice through the Looking Glass, but it is just as striking and sometimes even more illuminating than the time domain. In this

Box 1.5 Wave Motion

Waves can be described by a few parameters. Consider the simple harmonic wave drawn as a solid line below with wave height y at a particular position x and time t. Suppose the maximum *amplitude* of the wave is A and the *wavelength* λ (Greek lambda) is the distance between the crests.

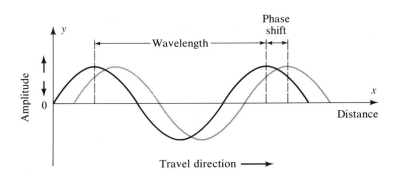

The time for a complete wave (e.g., crest to crest) to travel one wavelength is called the *period T*. Thus the wave velocity v is

$$v = \lambda/T \tag{1}$$

The frequency of the wave f is the number of complete waves that pass every second so that

$$f = 1/T \tag{2}$$

The actual position of a wave depends on its position relative to the origin of time and distance. Consider the light line in the figure. This wave is ahead of the first wave by a distance Δx. It is said to be *out of phase* by this amount.

Finally, the traveling simple harmonic wave can be described mathematically as

$$y = A \sin \frac{2\pi}{\lambda}(vt + x + \Delta x) \tag{3}$$

alternative frame, we need to be familiar with the concepts of wave frequency, wave period, and wavelength. These are defined in Box 1.5. This box shows two simple harmonic waves in the time domain. In the illustration, they both have the same amplitude, frequency, and wavelength; they differ in phase only. Of course, with earthquakes, we are dealing with a mix of waves of different amplitudes, frequencies, wavelengths, and phases; these ingredients make up the technicolor world of changing wave patterns.

In some ways, the picture through the time window is deceptively simple, and if we ever wish to look at each ingredient of the total wave pattern, we must have a way to separate the various wave types. The frequency domain allows this separation. The frequency window shows a spectrum of waves of different frequencies that make up the total motion. Although not as common as the time display, there are everyday examples of such wave spectra. The most familiar is the rainbow spectrum, first explained correctly by Isaac Newton, that is seen when a beam of sunlight passes through a glass prism in a darkened chamber. Newton found that the prism despersed the white light into the spectrum of primary colors (red, orange, yellow, green, blue, indigo, and violet). In other words, the simple wave components of white light were separated according to their frequencies, in this case because the amount of refraction of light depends on its color, i.e., upon its frequency. Over a century later, in 1807, the great French physicist Jean Baptiste Fourier showed that complex wave shapes can be regarded as the superposition of simple harmonic components, each with its own frequency, wavelength, and phase. From this basic idea the striking spectral pictures of the frequency domain are built.

Interpretation of the spectrum of waves and vibrations has become of immense importance in exploring the physical world. Many types of wave spectra from light, sound, earthquakes, and elsewhere have been used in inverse problems. On the microscopic atomic scale, "bright line" frequency spectra are characteristic of vibrating atoms, and they gave physicists the first understanding of the fine structure of the atom that lies outside of direct observation. As we will see in Chapter 6, bright-line spectra are also characteristic of the vibrations of the whole Earth, which occur after the occurrence of a great earthquake.

For another example of helpful visualization in the frequency domain, consider a case familiar to musicians. The wave shape of a sound produced by a piano string when struck is quite complicated. When transformed into the frequency domain by methods that need not detain us here (see Figures 6.2a and 6.2b) the complex sound is seen to be made up of a variety of simple pure tones. These tones are harmonics or overtones of the wave of lowest frequency present, called the fundamental. In acoustics, such sound analysis is commonplace, and it shows that any musical tone, no matter whether melodic or dissonant, is the sum of a finite number of simple harmonic waves of frequency of one, two, three, and so on, times that of the fundamental, each with its own amplitude and phase. In Chapter 6 of this book we will analyze in the same way the remote music of our own vibrating globe.

Normally, however, when a seismogram, such as Figure 3.4, is looked at through the frequency Looking Glass, its spectrum is seen to consist of a continuous band of energy over a wide range of frequencies. This analysis is analogous to Newton's prism experiment in which the color spectrum from white light has a continuous range extending from ultraviolet through the visible into infrared. The continuous frequency spectrum for earthquakes tells us that there is a variable amount of energy present at all frequencies. To simplify matters, we might when appropriate select only a limited frequency band by filtering out the earthquake waves having frequencies that are troublesome or of no interest.

The duality that we have outlined between the display of earthquake waves in terms of time and their display in terms of frequency provides the basic analytic tool for exploration of the Earth's interior. In the detective stories that follow, we will need to develop the skill to pass easily from one domain to the other if we are to gain full insight.

Harold Jeffreys (b. 1891)
*"If geophysics requires mathematics for its treatment,
it is the Earth that is responsible, not the
geophysicist."*

CHAPTER 2

Types of Earthquake Waves

Waves in Nature

In later chapters we will follow the waves that are generated in an earthquake down into the interior of the Earth. When they finally emerge at the surface we will encounter them as unidentified earthquake onsets, or UEO's. The Earth will be thought of as a giant lens with concentric layers of different properties. The passage of the seismic waves on their way to the surface again will be analogous to light traveling through this lens and focused by the layers.

In preparation for the journey to the center of the Earth we should first outline the properties of wave propagation that occur. It is convenient to look at wave properties in two ways: properties that depend on the essential wave nature of the traveling energy and those that depend essentially on the simple geometrical property that waves travel in straight lines in a homogeneous medium. The first description we will consider here and the second in the next section.

That light waves travel in straight lines is well known. The same property of rectilinear propagation enables us to speak of seismic *rays* in the Earth, which are the rectilinear paths along which the earthquake waves are propagated. From any seismic source, an infinite number of seismic rays can be drawn (see Figure 4.5) and a collection of these rays is called a *pencil* of seismic rays.

Familiar waves are sound in the air, waves on a body of water, waves along a rope, light through a lens, and so on. All these waves are simply energetic vibrations of the particular medium with certain amplitudes and frequencies.

When a piano string is struck by its hammer, for example, the vibrations of the string produce alternate compressions (pushes) and dilations (pulls) of the adjacent air, setting up sound waves. The more energetically it is struck, the greater the amplitude of the waves. Because the air is more or less uniform in elastic properties, the sound waves spread out as spherically expanding surfaces, with equal speed in all directions. Seismic waves through the rock of the interior have analogous properties.

A tuning fork produces a pure musical wave having a single frequency. For example, the frequency of middle C is 256 vibrations per second (256 Hertz). Above middle C on a key board, the sound wave frequency is greater, and below it the frequency is less. The same situation is found in seismology, where, as a start, we can think of the source of an earthquake in the same way as the hammer of a piano. When a geological fault ruptures, many seismic waves of different frequencies and amplitudes are generated, and if the fault rupture is energetic enough (a "great" earthquake) the whole Earth will vibrate in many frequencies like a piano string. A trained musical ear can distinguish between the complex tones emitted by one piano and those from another piano, because the overtones are produced in different combinations of amplitudes by the different instruments. In other words, the spectra of individual frequencies and amplitudes in complex tones are different and these differences can be recognized by the ear. As we will see, the analogy carries over to the Earth.

To understand further some of the basic wave aspects of earthquakes, let us next consider waves on the surface of water. From the disturbance caused by a stone thrown in a pond, a train of waves spreads out carrying energy toward the shore. The distance between the crests or troughs of water waves is variable. For ripples, the wavelength may be less than a centimeter, whereas in the deep oceans the distance between the wave crests may be hundreds of meters. (In the case of tsunamis, the name given to seismic sea waves produced by faulting of the ocean floor in earthquakes, wavelengths may be as great as 100 km.) As we watch the water waves spreading out on the pond, their amplitudes gradually decrease. This is simply because the initial energy is being spread out over a wider and wider area. For this reason, this type of decrease of wave amplitude is called attenuation by *geometrical spreading*. Geometrical spreading occurs also, of course, in the passage of seismic waves through the interior of the Earth, and it has an important effect on the detection of weak earthquake signals since the farther the waves spread, the more their amplitudes decrease, owing to the thinning out of energy.

Let us look again at the train of water waves on the pond. A careful watch will show that those ripples with the shortest wavelengths begin to pass ahead of the waves with longer wavelengths. After a time the train sorts itself out into a procession with the shorter waves traveling farther and farther ahead of the longer waves. This sorting of waves is called *dispersion,* in which the wave velocity is not a constant but depends upon the wavelength (or frequency) of the waves. Seismic waves have this property in common with water waves, and as we will explain in Chapter 4, dispersion of waves has been much used in determining properties of the Earth. An example of dispersed earthquake waves can be seen in Figure 3.4.

When the water waves in a pond encounter a barrier like a steep shoreline, they will reflect away from the shore, and an outgoing train of waves develops and passes through the ingoing train. We have all been fascinated to observe that as water waves wash against the end of a sharp obstacle or an opening between two obstacles, they bend, or are *diffracted,* into the quiet waters behind the obstacles (see Figure 8.1). With careful observation this diffraction of water waves can also be seen to be a function of the wavelengths. The longer waves are diffracted more into the quiet zone than the shorter ones. Like dispersion, diffraction is a wave property that can only be explained when the full wavelike character of waves is taken into account, because if we consider only wave energy passing along straight lines (as in the next section), we would predict that an obstacle would produce a sharp shadow. We would not be able to explain the presence of wave energy bent around into the shadow zone.

As well as with water waves diffraction is well known in acoustics and optics, and we can base our seismological discussion on these analogies. Because audible sound waves have much longer wavelengths than those of visible light, sound waves are diffracted around a corner much more than light waves. Thus we can hear conversations from around a corner when we cannot see the people who are talking. Inside the Earth, large obstacles such as the central nucleus block the passage of seismic waves, and as we will see in Chapter 5, seismic waves of long wavelength are diffracted markedly around these objects.

Water waves also provide a familiar example of the way that a medium moves as waves propagate through it. In the pond, as water waves pass by, a floating object is displaced up and down with the particles of the water. As swimmers in an ocean swell know, displacements near the surface of the swell are both horizontal and vertical. Beyond breaking surf, the crests carry a swimmer upward and forward at the same time, and in the trough a swimmer sinks and is pulled backward. The sum of these perpendicular motions is a circular motion which, after the wave has passed, leaves the swimmer more or less in the same place as before. A swimmer also knows that the circular motion is modified as he swims below the surface and, at depth, there is a region that is unaffected by the waves. Such water waves are called *surface waves* because they affect only the near surface fluid. As we will see below, certain earthquake waves are closely analogous.

By comparison with surface water waves, sound waves in the atmosphere only involve particles of air moving backward and forward in the direction in which the sound wave is moving. Such waves are called *compressional* and displace the medium always along the direction of propagation (see Figure 2.1(a)). A second category of wave motion that is simpler than that in surface waves occurs when a wave is sent down a rope by flicking the end. The wave travels down the rope as a series of crests and troughs with displacements at right angles to the direction of propagation of the wave along the rope. These waves move the particles of the medium as in Figure 2.1(b) and are called *transverse* waves. As we noted in Chapter 1, as early as 1897 R. D. Oldham spotted that both compressional and transverse waves (called *P* and *S* waves in seismology) occur in earthquakes and travel in the solid parts of the Earth's interior.

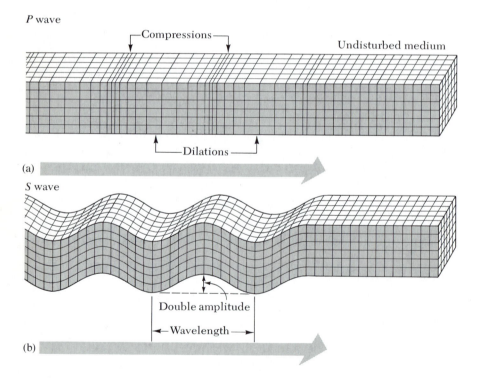

Figure 2.1   The two types of body waves. [From Bruce A. Bolt, *Nuclear Explosions and Earthquakes*. W. H. Freeman and Company. Copyright © 1976.]

Seismic Rays

We now return to the analogy between the Earth and a huge glass spherical lens used by R. D. Oldham in 1906 (see Box 1.2). As in the case of light waves, we make use of the concept of rays in following the paths of seismic waves through the Earth. In a medium with uniform properties, waves spread out from a point source with spherical fronts, and the transmitted energy can be regarded as rays moving outward along radii from the source. From an earthquake source, there-fore, a seismic ray can be drawn as a line through the interior of the terrestrial lens. If the refractive properties of the Earth were everywhere the same, such a *seismic ray,* like a light ray, would follow a straight line or chord, and we could think of the wave energy as passing along bundles of such straight rays at a fixed velocity. This was the assumption made by Oldham in 1906 and Lehmann in 1936 in calculations of the radii of the Earth's central and inner cores. However, to complicate matters a little, the velocity of seismic waves varies with depth inside the Earth. Broadly speaking, the deeper in the Earth a ray penetrates, the greater is the speed of the wave. Under these circumstances, the rays are curved with the concave side upward (see Figure 1.3).

Like light rays that encounter a water surface, seismic rays are governed by the laws of *reflection* and *refraction*. These laws are illustrated in Box 2.1. The law of reflection states that when the ray is reflected from the surface, the angle of incidence between the ray and the normal to the surface equals the angle between the normal and the reflected ray. That is, the reflected ray comes off the reflector, like a billiard ball, at the same angle as it hits.

The law of refraction governs the case when the ray passes obliquely from one medium in which it has one velocity to a medium in which it has another, such as when a ray of light passes from air into water. Under such circumstances, the direction of the transmitted ray is changed at the interface. The law of refraction was discovered in the seventeenth century by Willebrode Snell, and its mathe-matical form is given in Box 2.1. Simply stated, the amount of refraction depends upon the ratio of the wave velocities in the two media. For both the law of reflection and the law of refraction, the incident ray, the refracted ray, and the normal to the boundary surface all lie in the same plane.

A consequence of the law of refraction is that there is an angle of incidence called the *critical angle* for which the angle of refraction is 90 degrees. In this special case, energy from the refracted ray travels along the interface (see the lower diagram in Box 2.1). The resulting wave properties can be dealt with completely only by using the full wave theory of diffraction discussed in the last section, rather than in terms of rays. Such a treatment is, of course, beyond the

Box 2.1   Reflection and Refraction of Seismic Rays

Snell's Laws

Suppose a ray is incident on the boundary at O with angle of incidence i. There will, in general, be reflected and refracted rays.

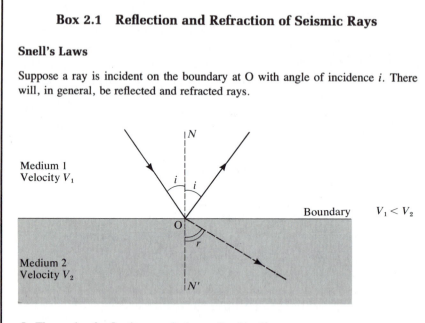

I. The angle of reflection equals the angle of incidence.
II. The angle of refraction r and the angle of incidence are related by

$$\frac{\sin i}{V_1} = \frac{\sin r}{V_2} \qquad (1)$$

where V_1, V_2 are the wave velocities in the two media as shown.

expectations of this book. When the angle of incidence is greater than the critical angle, no refracted rays appear in the other medium and the seismic ray is reflected totally internally. (Box 2.1 illustrates how this occurs.)

Now a ray property of the utmost importance. A consequence of Snell's law is that seismic rays in the Earth normally follow a path such that the time of travel from one point to another is *the least possible*. This crucial property holds irrespective of whether the ray encounters any reflecting or refracting surfaces on its way to the observing point. Sometimes, however, rays follow paths that are *maximum time paths* and interestingly enough, in a sphere like the Earth, sometimes a combination of the two. The property can be illustrated simply for an important case that will arise in the discussions of Chapter 5.

Critical Reflection and Refraction

Consider rays between the point F and the recorders R_0, R_1. The direct rays are FR_0 and FR_1. A reflected ray FAR_0 is also possible from the boundary. At R_1 no simple refracted ray that satisfies Snell's laws is possible for the angle of incidence i greater than the critical angle i_c.

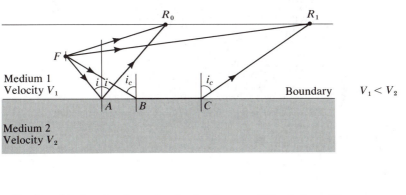

For the critical angle, the angle of refraction $r = 90°$ and, from (1),

$$\sin i_c = V_1/V_2 \qquad (2)$$

There is then a diffracted wave along the path $FBCR_1$.

Consider a diametrical plane through a simple model of the Earth that has constant velocity throughout, as shown in Figure 2.2. Let us follow a family of four separate rays starting at the point marked F, which is situated a little below the free surface of the sphere. Each of the four rays, after leaving F, arrives at the recording station R. One of the rays, called P, connects directly from F to R. The three remaining rays are all echoes that reach R after a single reflection at the surface. Because at any such reflection point the angle of incidence must equal the angle of reflection, it is not obvious that three separate reflecting points can be found; although we shall not trouble about the proof here, a little trigonometry proves that the three rays drawn in Figure 2.2 do in fact exist.

The first reflected ray, $F1R$, leaves the point F above the horizontal and travels

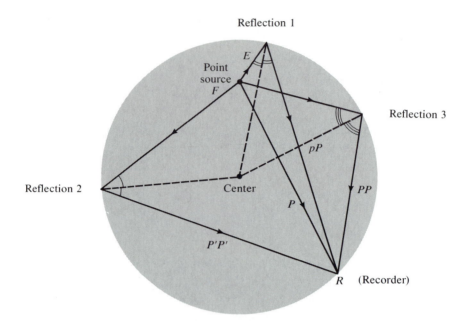

Figure 2.2 Seismic waves leaving the focus *F* at some depth in the Earth. There is one direct wave and three types of reflected waves. An upward ray is reflected at point 1 to the recorder *R* (designated *pP*). This is a minimum time path. The ray to point 2 and its reflection to the recorder is a maximum time path (*P'P'*). The third path is a maximum path in the plane of the page, but a minimum path if pulled outside this plane. This mini-max path goes from *F* to reflection point 3 and then to the recorder (*PP*).

to the surface near to the source point *F*. At the surface it is reflected at reflection point 1 back to *R*. This path turns out to be the fastest way that a ray that is once reflected at the surface can travel from *F* to *R*. Consider, now, the second reflected ray *F2R*. In this case, the ray leaves *F* well below the horizontal and travels to the reflection point 2 on the other side of the Earth, where it is reflected, according to Snell's law, to *R*. Measurement with a ruler will easily verify that this long path has the maximum length of all possible paths for an echo from *F* to *R*.

The third and most intriguing alternative is the ray echo from *F* to *R* by way of reflection point 3. It has the curious feature that if the reflection point 3 is moved in *the diametrical plane* a little toward *F* or *R*, the total path length decreases, so the path *F3R* is a maximum. Yet, if the reflection point is moved along the surface of the sphere *out of the diametrical plane* (i.e., out of the plane of the paper), the path length will increase. Thus, we can find variations in the path for which the travel time of the ray $F3R$ is either a minimum or a maximum. This type of ray path is called a *mini-max*.

The simple description that we have given above finds important application to seismic rays in the Earth. The point F can be identified with the center of the earthquake source, termed the *focus*. In this case, the focus is at considerable depth below the surface, and such an earthquake is conveniently called a deep-focus earthquake. In such an event, we can expect to get seismic waves traveling along the ray paths shown in Figure 2.2 and be recorded in order by a seismograph at the station R. It is clear enough that if F were on the surface, there would be only two reflected rays since we could not have the upward reflection $F1R$. Even more important, for a deep focus the backward echo $F1R$ will be a sensitive measure of the depth of the earthquake source. In observational practice, the difference in travel time between the direct ray FR and the upward reflection $F1R$ is the most precise way available to determine the focal depths of earthquakes (see Chapter 5 and Figure 5.2).

Seismic Waves Traveling Through the Earth

The musical sounds and acoustic waves that we discussed in the first section of this chapter propagate in all types of media—gases, liquids, and solids. As illustrated in Figure 2.1, all sound waves are transmitted by alternative compressions and dilations of the media, so that the vibrations are longitudinal, i.e., in the direction of travel like the opening and closing of a coiled spring.

Further it is evident enough that, in a gas or a liquid, compressional waves are the *only* waves that can propagate, because media such as air or water cannot sustain shear motions. On the other hand, this restriction does not hold for an elastic solid, and in the solid part of the Earth two types of waves can propagate. This physical property was known to Oldham in 1897 when he made his famous identification of the first and second preliminary tremors on seismograms (see Chapter 1). The fleetest of these is the *primary* wave or P wave. It is a sound wave that propagates by pulling and pushing on the elastic rocks, and it can travel through both liquid and solid parts of the Earth's interior. The second type of elastic wave, which can travel only in solids, is the *secondary* wave or S wave. These waves may be thought of as "shake waves" because they propagate by vibration of the particles of the rock at right angles to the direction of travel, like an oscillating violin string. The mode of motion is illustrated in Figure 2.1. In the Earth, the solid rocks are sheared and twisted as the S wave travels through

Box 2.2   Properties of Seismic Waves

The elasticity of a homogeneous, isotropic solid can be defined by two constants, k and μ. For a liquid, μ is zero.

k is the modulus of incompressibility or bulk modulus
  for granite, $k \simeq 27 \times 10^{10}$ dynes/cm^2 (270 kbars)
  for water, $k \simeq 2.0 \times 10^{10}$ dynes/cm^2 (20 kbars)

μ is the modulus of rigidity
  for granite, μ is about 1.6×10^{11} dynes/cm^2 (160 kbars)
  for water, $\mu = 0$

Body Waves

Within the body of an elastic solid with density ρ, two elastic waves can propagate with velocities α and β:

P *waves*   velocity $\alpha = \sqrt{(k + \frac{4}{3}\mu)/\rho}$

  for granite, $\alpha = 5.5$ km/sec
  for water, $\alpha = 1.5$ km/sec

S *waves*   velocity $\beta = \sqrt{\mu/\rho}$
  for granite, $\beta = 3.0$ km/sec
  for water, $\beta = 0$ km/sec

them, but because a liquid cannot be sheared, no S waves stray into the liquid regions.

In strong surface rocks, like granite, the velocity of P waves is typically about 5.5 km/sec and that of S waves is about 3 km/sec. In the deep interior, as the rocks become compressed, the measurements of the time of travel of seismic P and S waves along known distances show that the rocks at depth have velocities in excess of 11 km/sec for P waves and of 7 km/sec for S waves. (Table 3 in the Appendix gives estimated P and S wave velocities inside the Earth.)

The actual speed of seismic waves is dependent on the elastic properties and densities of the rocks through which they pass. The forms of the dependencies, which are fortunately uncomplicated, are given in Box 2.2. It turns out that the velocity of P waves depends upon the resistance of the rock to compression (the

When incident on a boundary, a seismic body wave will generate reflected and/or refracted waves of *both P* and *S* types.

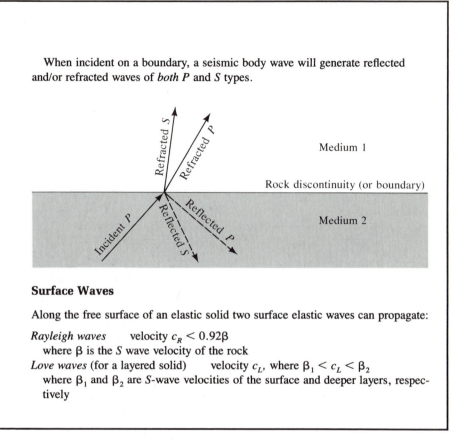

Surface Waves

Along the free surface of an elastic solid two surface elastic waves can propagate:

Rayleigh waves   velocity $c_R < 0.92\beta$
  where β is the S wave velocity of the rock
Love waves (for a layered solid)   velocity c_L, where $\beta_1 < c_L < \beta_2$
  where β_1 and β_2 are S-wave velocities of the surface and deeper layers, respectively

modulus of incompressibility), the resistance to twisting (the modulus of rigidity), and the density. The velocity of S waves depends only on the last two of these elastic parameters. (Remember you cannot twist a liquid but you can compress it.) By means of these formulas in Box 2.2, measurements of P and S speeds in the Earth yield values for ratios of elastic incompressibility and rigidity to density. These values are by far the most important data available to us on the properties of the terrestrial interior, and recent estimates are given in Tables 4 and 5 of the Appendix.

In this book, we will not go into the full mathematical detail that enables these elastic ratios to be computed, although we will discuss the general approach in Chapter 7. Suffice to say here that the estimation of these properties constitutes one of the major accomplishments of seismological research to date. In the first ten years of the century, scientists like Milne and Oldham had only a very rough idea of the P and S velocities throughout the Earth and of incompressibility, rigidity, and density values. By the early 1940's, all these quantities had been estimated quite closely by some of the outstanding scientists who worked in seismology: K. E. Bullen, Beno Gutenberg, and Sir Harold Jeffreys.

Because an earthquake source produces both S and P waves, encounters with seismic waves from the Earth's interior are somewhat more complicated than the study of sound waves in the atmosphere or light waves in a lens. Because both light and S waves are transverse vibrations, they have one property in common that is not possessed by sound or P waves, both longitudinal waves. Although both P and S waves exhibit reflection and refraction at boundaries and diffraction effects at corners and edges of obstacles, only S waves exhibit the phenomenon called *polarization*.

The polarization of light is familiar to anyone who has benefited from polarized eyeglasses to cut down on scattered light. A polarized lens has the property that only those light waves that are vibrating transversely in certain planes (up and down, horizontally, etc.) can pass through. The transmitted light waves are said to be plane-polarized. Sunlight coming through the atmosphere is not polarized in the sense that there is no preferred transverse direction of vibration of the light waves. However, by interaction with reflecting surfaces such as the ocean surface, or by refraction by crystals, or by passing through specially prepared plastic as in Polaroid eyeglasses, this unpolarized light can be made to be plane-polarized with a single plane of vibration.

We have an exact analog for S waves in earthquakes. As S waves travel through the Earth, they encounter structural discontinuities that refract or reflect them and polarize their vibrations. When an S wave is polarized so that the particles of rock move only in a horizontal plane, it is denoted by the symbol SH. When the particles of rock all move in the vertical plane containing the direction of propagation, the S wave is called an SV wave. As we will see in Chapters 3 and 5, the polarization properties of S waves affect the design of seismographs and the interpretation of seismograms, and provide clues on hidden structures.

There is a unique happening when seismic waves are incident on a reflecting surface within the Earth. Nothing like it occurs with sound, light, or water waves. A P wave, for example, hitting a boundary surface at an angle breaks up, as illustrated in Box 2.1, into *both* a reflected P wave and a refracted P wave. *As well, however, it generates a reflected S wave and a refracted S wave.* The reason is that at the point of incidence the rock at the boundary is not only being compressed but also sheared.

In other words, an incident P wave results in four transformed waves. This proliferation of wave types is sketched in Box 2.2. The same conversion of one wave type to another occurs when an *SV* wave hits an internal boundary obliquely; both reflected and refracted *P* and *SV* waves result. A little thought on the way that the rock particles move transversely in a vertical plane as the incident *SV* wave approaches will indicate in this case that both the reflected and refracted *S* waves are always of *SV* type. By contrast, if the incident *S* wave is of the horizontally polarized *SH* type, so that the particles are moving backward and forward out of the plane but parallel to the surface of the boundary, there will be no compressions or vertical displacements produced at the discontinuity. Therefore, because these are needed to generate new *P* and *SV* waves, respectively, there is only one reflected and one refracted wave, both of *SH* type. By similar elementary reasoning, when a *P* wave is incident *normal to a reflecting boundary,* there is no component of shear at the surface so that there is only a reflected *P* wave and no reflected *SV* or *SH* waves at all. This restriction is a vital one for a case that we will explore in Chapter 7.

As they are the keys to the Earth's interior, we must now give the simple notation used to describe the various types of *P* and *S* rays in the Earth. Through such notations we hope to identify ultimately the many UEO's that we encounter. Reflections and refractions of *P* and *S* waves at the Earth's surface and its subterranean boundaries produce whole families of seismic rays and, if the corresponding wave onsets are to be named on seismograms, a simple nomenclature is needed for quick identification. The standard one is illustrated in Figure 2.3.

First, rays that travel directly without reflection between the focus F and the recorder at the seismographic stations are designated by the single symbol *P* or *S* when the ray segment lies entirely in the mantle. Any ray segment of *P* waves that lies in the outer core is labeled *K* (from the German *Kernwellen,* for core waves), and any segment of *P* type in the inner core is labeled *I*. Thus, the symbol *PKIKP* corresponds to a wave that starts in the mantle as a *P* wave, is refracted into the outer core as a *P* wave (*K* leg), is refracted through the inner core as a *P* wave (*I* leg), refracted back out into the outer core as a *P* wave (second *K* leg), and is finally refracted back into the mantle as *P*. Sometimes, for short, *PKP* is simply written as *P'* (see Box 1.4). There is no symbol corresponding to *K* for *S* waves, because *S* waves have not been found that have passed through the outer core. A symbol *J,* however, has been adopted for *S* waves with paths through the inner core. (As we will see in Chapter 4, there is evidence that the inner core of the Earth is solid.)

As shown in Figure 2.3, waves are also reflected at the outer surface. Reflected *P* waves with two legs are called *PP,* with three *PPP,* and so on. In the same way, we have *SS, SSS,* etc., for one, two, and more reflections of *S* waves. Because of the conversion from one wave type to another on reflection discussed

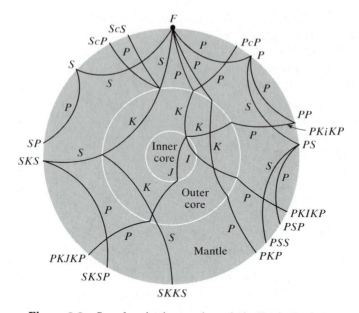

Figure 2.3 Sample seismic rays through the Earth. Begin at the focus of the earthquake *F*. The symbol *c* designates a wave reflected at the outer core's surface; thus *PcP* is a *P* wave through the mantle reflected at the core; *PcS* is a *P* wave reflected as *S*. The symbol *i* designates a wave reflected at the inner core's bundary: *PKiKP*. The symbols *K* and *I* refer, respectively, to *P* waves that have traveled through the outer and inner core. The symbol *SP* designates an *S* wave through the mantle reflected at the surface as *P*. *PKS* travels through mantle and core as *P*, and up through the mantle again as *S*. The ray marked *PKJKP*, which travels as *S* through the inner core, has not been observed.

above, we denote, for example, by *SP*, the wave that has its first leg as *S* and the second as *P*. As straightforward extensions we have *PPS*, *SKSP*, and so on.

We have already referred to the reflected rays that arise in deep-focus earthquakes. By comparing Figures 2.2 and 2.3, we can identify the direct ray *P*, and the three reflections *PP*, *P'P'* (assuming the longest path goes through the core), and the unique case called *pP*. In the last case, the use of the lowercase prefix *p* denotes the ray leg that has ascended from the focus to the outer surface as a *P* wave. We thus can list the whole group of near-focus reflections *pP*, *sP*, *pS*, and *sS*. In the second case, for example, the wave has traveled upward as an *S* wave on a short leg, and has then bounced back at the surface as a wave of *P* type.

These particular waves are prized in seismology for their ability to fix the focal depths of earthquakes and to prospect for the dipping structures under island arcs (see Chapter 5 and Figure 5.3).

As a shorthand, various letters and numbers can be inserted between the two (or more) *P*'s and *S*'s to indicate specifically the number of reflections the wave has suffered or the boundary from which it has been reflected. Thus, a compressional wave that has been reflected once inside the outer boundary of the core is called *PKKP*; if reflected twice, the symbol is *PKKKP*, and so on. Recently, *P* waves have been detected that have been reflected up to 13 times at the underside of the mantle-core boundary (see Figure 4.5). These are called *PmKP*, where $m - 1$ is the number of reflections in the core. We will discuss the implications of these extraordinary multiple echoes in Chapter 4 (see Figure 4.6). Much of our story will be about such echoes from boundaries deep down in the planet.

The important seismic waves that are reflected from the outside of the boundary of the outer core are called *PcP*, *PcS*, and *ScS*. The small letter *c* indicates an outward reflection at the core boundary. The companion symbol *i* denotes upward reflection at the surface of the inner core and so we write *PKiKP* for the inner core echo of wholly *P* type.

The intermediate symbol *d* (or its value in kilometers) is inserted between *PP*, *SS*, *P'P'*, etc. to denote the depth of a boundary below the surface from which a seismic ray is reflected downward. Sample rays of this type are drawn in Figure 4.3. For example, the symbol *P400P* specifies a *PdP* wave that has been reflected at the *underside* of a boundary at a depth of 400 km. The symbol *h* is used to denote waves that may be reflected from discontinuities around the inner core of the Earth, giving rise to such combinations as *PKhKP*.

Finally, our catalog needs to include a notation for diffracted waves. Because in the following account we will only consider wave diffraction associated with the core, we will need only the notation *dif P* and *dif S*. Waves with these names refer to the *P* and *S* waves that creep around the boundary between the Earth's mantle and core. As we will see, these diffracted waves contain valuable information on the detail of structural changes at the base of the mantle (see, for the corresponding *dif P* and *dif S* rays, the diagrams in Figures 1.3 and 4.3).

This notation for the various *P* and *S* waves is summarized in Table 6 in the Appendix for easy reference.

The reader might initially feel that with such a multitude of possible seismic rays, it would be extremely difficult to tag a particular ray quantitatively throughout its path. Fortunately, this is not so. Indeed, only *one* parameter is needed to identify a ray (see Box 2.3) and once this number is specified the ray can be followed from earthquake source to seismographic station.

Box 2.3   Parameters of Rays in the Earth

In the Earth, seismic P and S waves follow curved paths FS. At every point along the ray, Snell's law, given in Box 2.1, holds. For rays in a sphere, relation (1) in Box 2.1 is modified to

$$\frac{r_Q \sin i_Q}{V_Q} = \frac{R \sin i_s}{V_s} = \text{constant} = p \qquad (1)$$

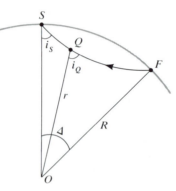

Here, V is the P (or S) velocity at any point Q of a ray, distant r from the Earth's center O. The angle of incidence at Q is i_Q.

N.B. The ray parameter p in (1) is constant along the entire ray. However, it is different for other rays of the same type that leave F.

The travel times T from F to S depend upon the angle SOF, called Δ, at the center of the sphere, i.e., the angles subtended by the ray at O. For a small increase $d\Delta$ in the angle Δ there is, in general, a small increase dT in the travel time T.

The ray parameter p can be shown to be given by

$$p = \frac{dT}{d\Delta} \qquad (2)$$

N.B. The value of p above is the slope, at the appropriate distance Δ, of the travel-time curve for the ray in question (see Box 3.2). The units of p are thus seconds of time per degree of arc. ($1° \simeq 110$ km for the Earth.)

Seismic Waves Traveling
Along the Surface

We saw in Chapter 1 that the early seismograms showed not only "preliminary tremors," identified as P and S waves, through the body of the Earth, but also "large waves," which came later and had considerable amplitude and duration. These waves were soon identified as waves that travel around the surface of the Earth. One helpful way to think of these surface waves is as wave motion that is guided by the outer boundary like sound waves are guided around a "whispering gallery."*

In surface waves, most of the wave motion is located at the outside surface itself and the wave amplitudes decrease overall below the surface. Two main types of surface waves propagate in the Earth, and these are illustrated in Figure 2.4.

---

*Like the dome of St. Paul's Cathedral, London.

(a) Love wave

(b) Rayleigh wave

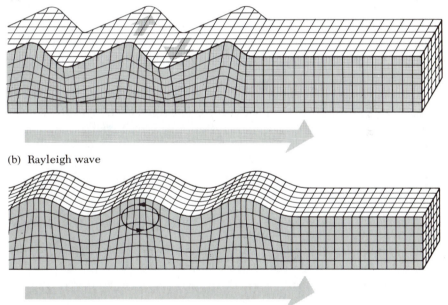

Figure 2.4   Ground motion at the Earth's surface: Love waves and Rayleigh waves. [After Bruce A. Bolt, *Nuclear Explosions and Earthquakes*. W. H. Freeman and Company. Cropyright © 1976.]

Love waves, named after the Cambridge mathematician, A. E. H. Love, who first described them, are the simpler. In Love waves, the ground moves from side to side in a horizontal plane but at right angles to the direction of propagation; there is no vertical motion. Another way to describe Love waves is as the sum of many polarized *SH* waves (see previous section) trapped near the surface of the Earth.

The second type of surface waves is the Rayleigh wave, again named after a famous British mathematician, Lord Rayleigh. In Rayleigh waves, the particles of rock vibrate both up and down and backward and forward following in effect an elliptical orbit. However, as shown in Figure 2.4, the elliptical orbit is restricted to a vertical plane pointed in the direction in which the waves are traveling. Rayleigh waves have no *SH* type motions at right angles to the direction of travel.

The two surface waves are thus seismic companions but with separate and distinguishable features. When encountered on a seismogram as a UEO, a Love wave can be distinguished from a Rayleigh wave in two ways. The first clue is given by the different particle motions described above. A seismogram showing only the vertical component of ground displacement can never record a Love wave with its pure *SH* motion. But vertical-component seismograms may contain Rayleigh surface waves. The second clue is the relative speed of the waves. Both types of surface waves travel slower than *P* and *S* waves propagating between the same points, but Love waves generally travel faster than Rayleigh waves (see Box. 2.2). In the next chapter we will use these decoding devices to unravel an actual seismogram.

Before leaving the subject of earthquake waves that roll across the terrestrial surface, we must stress that much general information about the Earth's outer parts has been gleaned from studying surface waves. Such studies depend upon the correlation between the length of a wave and the depth that it probes (see Box 2.4). Surface waves typically become dispersed out into long trains of waves as they travel around the Earth's surface. This sorting out of the waves according to period depends upon the variation of the elastic properties (modulus and density) with depth in the Earth. The waves with longer wave lengths travel faster because they penetrate to profounder depths.

Nowadays computers easily measure the phase of each component wave (defined in Box 1.4) that makes up an observed surface wave at a specific time at the earthquake observatory. From the phases, we can determine the position of a wave peak at a given time for each harmonic component at the station, or the number of peaks between two stations along the same wave path. Hence a wave speed, called the phase velocity, can be calculated which, when plotted against the corresponding wave frequency (or alternatively, wave period), yields curves such as those in Box 2.4. The position and shape of the graphed *dispersion curves* contain the information on deep structure and properties. Again we are faced with one of the fascinating inverse problems. If we knew what the properties of the Earth were, say under oceans or a particular continent, we could, from the known theory of surface waves, calculate the corresponding dispersion curve. Actually, we have an observed but cryptic curve and we want to infer the hidden properties. The reader should be warned that full enlightenment on surface wave dispersion across tectonically complex regions is not yet at hand, and the problem continues to engage both observational and theoretical seismologists. Unfortunately, because of limits of space, we will have to forego any further account of the way the Earth is probed with surface waves. We will, however, look at a closely related tool in the next section and in Chapter 6.

Standing Seismic Waves

Waves have a dual nature. We have so far found it convenient to speak of earthquakes propagating from the focus to the seismographic stations. But when a seismic wave is reflected back on itself at a boundary, the incoming and outgoing waves will add to produce a pattern of stationary or *standing* waves. Similarly, two trains of surface waves traveling in opposite directions around the spherical Earth will add together at the antipodes and produce a pattern of standing vibrations.

This duality between traveling waves and standing waves is often observed in nature. The concept is explained in Figure 2.5. In (a), a wave is traveling (along a string, say) from right to left. We can produce the same shape by adding together the two waves in (b) that are vibrating up and down as shown by the arrows. In the same way, the wave traveling from left to right in (c) is identical with the superposition of the two standing waves in (d).

For the musically minded, think of the waves in Figure 2.5 as resulting from the plucking of a violin string. Plucking produces musical tones composed of a fundamental tone and overtones or harmonics of the string. These tones are nothing but sound waves produced by sets of waves in the string. We can conceive of the string motions just as easily either as waves that travel back and forward along the string after reflections at the ends or as standing vibrations of the string transverse to its length. In the example of Figure 2.5, the two standing waves are the fundamental and first harmonic of the string, displaced so that they have a special phase relation with each other (indicated by the arrows).

Box 2.4   Displacements and Velocities of Love Waves

Displacement Curves

The figure shows the patterns of displacement with depth in three kinds (modes) of
Love wave for a period of 30 seconds. These modes correspond to the overtones of
a vibrating string (see Box 6.1). Although there are differences in the variation in
displacement with depth, in all cases the displacement ultimately becomes zero.

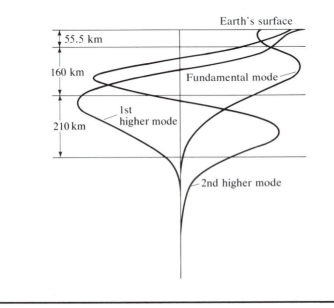

If we had a supersensitive movie camera mounted in an orbiting satellite we
could follow what happens to the seismic waves from the onset of an earthquake
to the establishment of global standing waves. (More realistically, in Figure 3.5
we follow pictorially the reflected *P* and *S* waves and surface waves for some time
during their fleeting history.) Imagine a large earthquake in which the transient
pulses have spread in all directions around the globe and the complex system of
traveling *P* and *S* waves and surface waves have intermingled to form a stationary
interference pattern of standing waves in the Earth. The appropriate description
of these standing waves is then given by the theory of vibrations.

Dispersion Curves

Dispersion curves for Love waves that propagate in their fundamental mode across oceans and across continents are shown below. The velocities would be different for different modes. Wave velocities at various periods are theoretical values calculated for the Pacific Ocean and California.

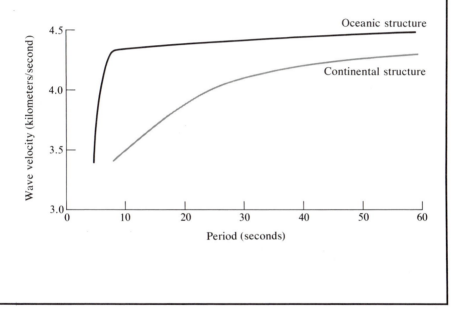

Finally, we should note that the dual property of waves described above is another aspect of the complementary worlds of time and frequency that were discussed in Chapter 1. Traveling waves are inhabitants of the world seen through the time window; standing waves are creatures of the frequency window and go hand in hand with spectral displays. Both descriptions yield valuable prizes of understanding of the middle of the Earth. In Chapters 4 and 5, we will deal mainly with the traveling waves, while in Chapter 6 we will switch to standing waves. Our sketch here is only qualitative and for a more basic treatment the reader must consult texts in the Guide to Further Reading.

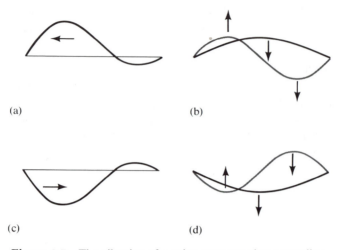

(a)   (b)

(c)   (d)

Figure 2.5   The vibration of a string represented as a traveling wave (a,c) or as two standing waves (b,d). Any wave motion, even the most complex, can be represented as the sum of a large number of modes.

Scattering and Dimming

As we noted earlier, using rays to follow seismic waves through the Earth provides a simple method of exploring the structure of the interior. We have also warned that rays can give inadequate description of certain wave behavior, such as diffraction, that occurs whenever there are rapid changes in the properties of the transmitting media. An important case is that of small-scale irregularities or obstacles that scatter the earthquake energy.

We can think of such obstacles reflecting back some of the energy externally and refracting some of it internally. The waves and the obstacles interact with the production of new waves that are scattered outward into the surrounding rock in all directions. The analogous scattering for water waves can be readily seen by watching the secondary ripples generated by buoys bobbing up and down in the incoming waves. Such observations show that the types of scattering depend upon the size of the obstacles relative to the wavelength of the incident waves. The general rule is that the longer the wave compared to the size of the obstacle, the less the wave is scattered by the obstacle.

This rule explains why the sky is blue. Sunlight, which contains many wavelengths (i.e., wave frequencies), is scattered by the air molecules and dust in the atmosphere. Because these particles are very small, compared with the wavelengths of visible light, the light with the short wavelengths (blue) is much more strongly scattered than the light of longer wavelengths. Thus, when we look up into the clear sky, it is mainly scattered blue light that catches the eye.

We need to describe one further effect before we leave this short review of waves. The farther we go from the source of light the dimmer is the room; the fury of ocean waves dies out at the edge of the storm; and we hear only faintly the throbbing of a distant drum. In all these cases, as with seismic waves, the energy in the wave becomes more thinly spread out as the wave front spreads out through a greater and greater volume.

One reason for the diminution of the wave amplitudes as the distance traveled increases is called *geometrical spreading* as mentioned earlier in the case of water waves, because it is produced only by geometrical effects. It is easy to show that the decrease in amplitude of the P and S waves through the body of the Earth is inversely proportional to the distance away from the focus. In comparison, surface wave amplitudes decrease inversely as the square root of the distance from the source. In neither case does the wave attenuation depend on the wavelengths.

We thus can explain the observations of von Rebeur Paschwitz (frontispiece). As the distance from the earthquake focus grows, the surface waves ("large waves") will become more and more prominent compared with the P and S waves ("preliminary tremors") because of the difference in geometrical spreading. A more modern example is given in Figure 3.4.

Of course, the energy in seismic waves dims also from other causes. For instance, scattering and reflection of waves by irregularities inside the Earth will cut down the transmitted amplitudes, and there is damping due to frictional resistance of the rocks to vibrations. Some of the wave energy is lost as heat, and this loss produces an amplitude decay as the earthquake progresses through the slightly inelastic rocks. Deep in the Earth's interior, frictional attenuation of seismic waves is found to be, in general, small but nevertheless measurable. While it is thus a nuisance to the observer by reducing the size of the seismic signal, frictional damping of the seismic waves tells us something about the nonelastic or plastic properties of the Earth's interior. In Chapter 6 we will indicate how the damping of earthquake vibrations is measured fairly closely by a single parameter, called Q. We will find that, like the speeds of P and S waves, the value of Q varies with depth, and it will be interesting to speculate on what these variations are telling us.

Ray Pictures by Computers

Nowadays elegant pictorial representations of seismic rays passing through complicated underground structures can be drawn by computer plotters. We give
several examples later in this book, such as Figure 4.5. Another fine specimen
is Figure 2.6.

Although it is possible in principle for a draftsman to make such ray pictures,
he would have to be supplied with the correct angles to draw the rays as they
reflect and refract from a particular boundary. Thus, much tedious arithmetic
would have to be done before the draftsman could even commence his work. But,
because of the high speed of digital computers, many, many rays with the correct
directions can be calculated rapidly and drawn directly. It is therefore feasible to
step off a family of rays at equal angles from their source, such as an earthquake
focus, and trace each ray through to the surface. Not only are the resulting
pictures visually artistic, they also provide much detail about the areas on the
surface of the Earth where seismic energy will be concentrated or diminished.

In Figure 2.6, the rays have been drawn by a computer to represent the transit
of seismic P-wave energy from an underground nuclear explosion in the Nevada
desert, westward under the Sierra Nevada and the Great Valley of California to
stations along the California coast, such as Berkeley. The diagram represents a

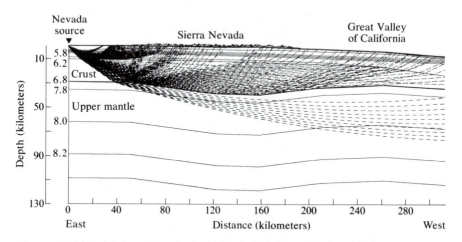

Figure 2.6   A computer plot of seismic P rays leaving a seismic focus in Nevada and
traveling through the crust and upper mantle to points on the surface to the west in
California. This crustal structure models the mountain root under the Sierra Nevada.
The numbers to the left are the seismic P velocities in the layer immediately above the
adjacent boundary.

postulated structure under the great mountain range. What is remarkable is that the pencil of rays, although they leave the source at successively equal angles, bunches up into intense bundles of energy in some regions and opens out in other regions, producing zones through which no seismic energy propagates.

This particular study is a portion of one being carried out by R. Gutdeutsch of the University of Vienna and myself in an attempt to understand the structure under the Sierra Nevada in California. As early as 1938, Perry Byerly at Berkeley had developed, using simple earthquake probes, a model for the crustal structure of central California, which had a mountain "root" under the Sierra Nevada. The crustal root in Figure 2.6 is represented by a thickening of the crust under the mountains down to depths of about 40 km, whereas the crust under the Great Valley of California extends down only to less than 30 km. The attraction of such ray diagrams is that they can be used to design field experiments in which instruments are properly placed to check whether wave intensities predicted by a favorite model actually occur. This application is only one illustration of the way that computers have become a powerful tool in probing the body of the Earth.

Beno Gutenberg (1889–1960)
"The first attempt to find the structure of the whole Earth from transmission times of earthquake waves through the Earth was made by R. D. Oldham."

CHAPTER 3

Measurements of Earthquake Waves

Earthquake Geography

The first glittering reward from a far-flung network of seismographic observatories around the world pioneered by John Milne (see Chapter 1) at the turn of the century was an unbiased picture of the distribution of the world's earthquakes. Knowledge of major seismicity last century was restricted mostly to earthquakes felt on the continents. Gradually, as this century waxed, *instrumental* earthquake location based on a global seismograph network bore fruit; today we have uniform maps such as Figure 3.1, which shows the positions of over 30,000 earthquakes recorded between 1963 and 1977. This splendid observational accomplishment by seismologists has depended upon universal cooperation in exchanging travel times of seismic waves by seismographic observatories. In 1980, there were some 2000 of these involved in international data exchange.

Excellent treatments of the meaning of these intriguing global patterns of earthquake activity, with their concentrated belts and nonseismic areas, have been published in recent years (see the Guide to Further Reading), so this aspect of seismology will not be pursued here. We should stress, however, that from studies of global seismicity has come crucial evidence on present geodynamics and deformation of the Earth. They have thrown much light on the puzzles of mountain building, the spreading of the sea floor, and the stresses on great tectonic plates. In this book, we focus on the deeper parts of the Earth; it would carry us too far afield to explore the tectonic causes of earthquakes. We do want to know,

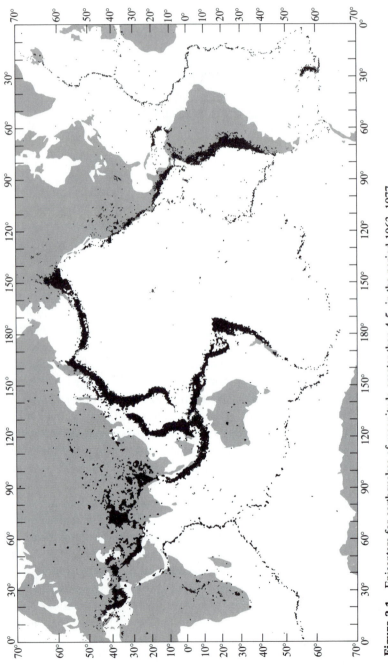

Figure 3.1 Epicenters for earthquakes of magnitude greater than 4.5, in the period 1963–1977. [Map computer plotted by Peter W. Sloss of NGSDC.]

however, where earthquake sources occur so that the need for crafty selection of sources of seismic waves for probing underground structure can be seen.

In the first place, Figure 3.1 shows that the distribution of natural earthquakes is by no means ideal. We would like to be able to select a source of earthquake waves anywhere on the surface of the Earth, particularly because seismographic observatories thus far are restricted to continental areas and a few islands. But the great aseismic continental shields like Siberia, Canada, Africa, Brazil, Antarctica, and Australia, and the vast abyssal plains of the oceans are almost free of earthquakes, so we must make do for most of our detective work with a limited distribution of seismic sources.

A by-product of the nuclear age has been the partial, but in some cases decisive, lifting of this geographical restriction by the underground detonation in the Pacific, Eurasia, and North America of large nuclear explosive devices. We will see in the next two chapters how such nuclear sources have been used as seismic probes.

Second, earthquakes are produced by sudden slip of geologic faults at various depths in the Earth. As noted earlier, the point from which the seismic waves first emanate is called the earthquake *focus* or *hypocenter*. The point on the Earth's surface vertically above the focus is called the *epicenter*. In natural earthquakes, the depth of the focus can range between a few kilometers down to depths of almost 700 km. However, the geographical regions of deep-focus earthquakes* are quite restricted. Most deep-focus earthquakes lie along present island arcs such as the Aleutian arc, the Japanese arc, the Marianas, the Tonga–Kermadec–New Zealand arc, Indonesia, the New Hebrides chain, and the Caribbean Antilles and the Aegean. There are also deep-focus earthquakes along continental margins where there are deep ocean trenches, such as under the South American Andes and Central America. Other deep-focus earthquakes occur under mountain chains like the Himalayas and Carpathians and under Spain. These deeper earthquakes have some precious observational advantages as sources of P and S waves. They often have simpler faulting slip mechanisms than shallow-focus earthquakes and produce simpler seismograms, which can be more easily correlated among different recording stations. Also, they give rise to unique sets of seismic rays, pP, sP, etc., associated with upward reflections near to the focus, which we defined in Figure 2.2.

We also need a yardstick against which to measure the size of an earthquake. Because we deal here only with recorded earthquakes, we need only mention the

---

*Deep-focus earthquakes were named and their reality established by K. Wadati in 1928.

most common *instrumental* method. Just as astronomers calculate the magnitude of a star, seismologists grade earthquakes according to seismic magnitude. The idea, due to the Japanese seismologist K. Wadati, and extended by Charles Richter in California in the early 1930's, is a relatively simple one. The amplitude of the largest seismic wave on a standard seismogram (from the Wood–Anderson seismograph) is measured with a ruler. Because this amplitude varies so enormously from tiny earthquakes to great ones, the logarithm of the measure is taken. This number is then used to enter a published table that gives the earthquake magnitude as a function of distance between the seismograph and the epicenter. Those interested in more details of the method will find them in a number of books in the Guide to Further Reading.

For our purposes, magnitude values of earthquakes and underground explosions will be mentioned in the following chapter solely to give a feel for the relative size, and hence energy, of the earthquake source. In fact, the magnitude scale has no upper or lower limit; the largest earthquakes recorded have Richter magnitudes of 8.5 to 8.9. The smallest earthquakes recorded by the most sensitive nearby seismographs have magnitudes of zero or even negative values. As probes to the deep interior, earthquakes with magnitudes between 6.0 and 7.5 are generally the best, since they usually provide the sharpest onsets of P and S waves and produce untangled surface wave trains. Greater earthquakes, however, are needed for energetic shaking of the whole Earth, as we will see in Chapter 6. Particularly valuable information, for instance, in recent years, was obtained from studies of the great 1960 Chilean earthquake and the 1964 Alaskan earthquake, both of magnitude 8.6.

Seismographs

Before taking a closer look at seismic readings and UEO's we must consider briefly the seismographic instruments that record the probing waves on seismograms. Most of these seismographs sense earthquakes by taking advantage of the inertia of a freely suspended mass.

Suppose we could float in the air quite unaffected by an earthquake. Then, we could make a seismogram by reaching down with a pencil and allowing it to move across a sheet of paper fastened to the shaking ground. However, because gravity prevents levitation, seismographs are designed with the central mass on an elastic suspension such as a spring, or a pendulum which suspends the mass by a hinge (see Figure 3.2). Such suspensions allow relative motions between the pendulum and the supporting frame fixed to the ground. When the supporting

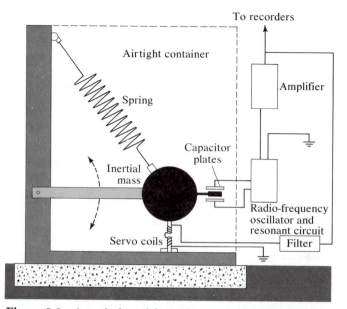

Figure 3.2   A vertical pendulum seismograph for detection of the vertical component of long earthquake waves. The mass tends to remain stationary as the Earth moves. Relative motion at the capacitor plates generates an electrical signal that is fed to an analogue and digital recorder. The filter feeds back spurious signals, representing motions other than those of the desired waves, to coils that keep the mass centered. [From Frank Press, "Resonant Vibrations of the Earth." Copyright © 1965 by Scientific American, Inc. All rights reserved.]

frame is shaken by the seismic waves, the inertia of the pendulum mass causes it to lag behind the motion of the frame (i.e., the ground waves and the recorded waves are out of phase).

These relative motions were once magnified by mechanical means but, nowadays, the tiny motions are boosted by electronic amplifiers. The electric signals generated by the motions are recorded by driving galvanometer mirrors or mechanical pens that produce a trace on sensitive paper, or they can be recorded directly onto magnetic tape and later the signal played back through some visual writing device.

Pendulums and springs have two special properties that were first hit upon by the great Italian physicist Galileo. First, a pendulum swings at a characteristic rate. The period for a single oscillation is quite independent of the amplitude of the oscillation as long as it does not become extreme. This remarkable fact is worth demonstrating by suspending a mass at the end of an elastic band, pulling it down and releasing it. The mass bobs up and down at a rate which depends only on the elastic properties of the elastic band. This resonant period of oscillation is referred to as an *eigenvibration* (from the German *eigen,* meaning "own"), and the frequency of this vibration is called the *eigenfrequency.* It is wholly a property of the system itself; any excitation of a pendulum or spring produces its eigenfrequency if it is subsequently left alone.

The second property of pendulums observed by Galileo is that when motion has started, oscillations continue at the eigenfrequency for a time dependent only upon the rate with which the energy is dissipated. The beats of a pendulum clock will continue at a constant rate as long as friction is compensated by the use of hanging weights. In the case of seismographs, the tendency of the pendulum to continue swinging after it has been set in motion by the earthquake must be controlled by some frictional device or by an electrical resistance or feed-back circuit. These devices counteract the pendulum's tendency to resonate excessively at its eigenfrequency. We are thus led to a seismograph design that looks something like Figure 3.2

It turns out that the most productive P and S earthquake waves for probing the Earth have periods between half a second and 20 seconds. On the other hand, the very long period eigenvibrations of the whole Earth produced in large earthquakes have periods up to one hour (see Chapter 6). In no other branch of physics is there such a great range in the frequency of the signals that are studied, and it should not be surprising that many different types of seismographs are needed.

Another complication in recording earthquakes is that the ground is in fact always in motion. This unceasing restlessness is called *microseismic noise.* Microseisms originate in the transfer of energy, from natural sources such as storms and wind and from human and industrial activity, into the oceans and continents. For high-fidelity resolution of faint earthquake signals, therefore, seismographs must be designed so that they are affected as little as possible by the unwanted microseisms. Mainly for this reason, it is common to operate different types of seismographs having different periods. For detection of the first and second preliminary tremors (the P and S waves), seismographs with free periods about 1 second are common. This is a higher natural frequency than the most common microseismic noise, which has periods of about 6 seconds. The most sensitive short-period seismographs can, at a quiet observatory site, detect ground displacements of a thousandth of a millionth of a meter. The visible record of such a signal might show a seismic wave amplitude of 1 centimeter, although the amplitude of the ground actually was 10^{-7} centimeters.

To detect longer period seismic waves such as surface waves, seismographs that magnify waves with periods of about 20 seconds are widely used. These intermediate seismographs can be modified by electronic circuits so that while they filter out the 6 second and even shorter period microseisms, they respond strongly to longer period waves.

A third type of seismograph is becoming more popular—one that has a long-period pendulum (free period sometimes greater than 20 seconds) and records a wide range of periods out to hundreds of seconds. Such instruments, called *broadband* seismographs, allow the recorded signals to be played back from magnetic tape through digital computers, thus displaying seismic waves in different frequency ranges at the experimenter's convenience.

The final component of a seismograph, but by no means the least important, is an accurate clock. Because the arrival times of the *P, S,* and surface waves that travel through the Earth must be reported on a common basis, all seismologists use Greenwich Mean Time (i.e., Universal Time) rather than local time for their time-keeping. Most modern earthquake observatories endeavor to keep their clocks correct to 1 millisecond continuously by checking them every day against the radio time signals transmitted by a standard world time service (such as WWV in the United States). In this way, the timing errors of many seconds, which were once endemic to travel-time studies of seismic waves such as those of Milne and Oldham in the early days of seismology, have been removed.

The usual complete seismograph consists of three components: the first senses the vertical motion of the ground and the other two respond to horizontal ground motions in two directions at right angles. Usually, but not always, the horizontal components are aligned so that they record the ground motion in a north-south direction and an east-west direction. The vertical component sensor of a seismograph (usually a mass suspended by springs as in Figure 3.2) gives the best recordings of the push-pull *P* waves, which arrive at a steep angle from deep in the Earth, and also of the Rayleigh surface waves. (Why?)

By contrast, the horizontal component sensors (usually horizontal pendulums) are able to record with fidelity waves with transverse or shear motion, such as *SH* and Love waves. Detective work on unidentified earthquake onsets is much simplified if all three directions of ground motion are faithfully recorded, because this enables reconstruction of the complete ground wave motion to be made and, often, sharp distinctions between UEO's.

Earthquake Observatories and Arrays

Just as modern astronomy depends upon a variety of sophisticated optical and radio telescopes, a modern well-equipped earthquake observatory has a variety of seismographs. Ideally these will be able to record the vertical and two horizontal components of the wave motion arriving at the station from remote sources over a very wide spectrum of frequencies.

Whenever possible, seismographs are sited carefully so that the microseisms that mask the UEO's are as small as possible. One quiet station in the United States that is remote from the ocean waves of the coastline and the works of man is Jamestown, part of the University of California network. It was set up by the author in 1964 on hard rock in an abandoned mineshaft in the western foothills of the Sierra Nevada. There the average microseismic ground movement has an amplitude of only 10 nanometers (10^{-6} cm). In this book, a number of examples of seismic waves that have traveled as faint echoes from the deep interior to the Jamestown station are reproduced (see Figure 4.6).

Routine work at a seismographic station begins with changing the photographic paper, film, or magnetic tapes each morning so that analysis of the previous day's records can commence. The analysis is done by a seismologist who selects the onsets on the seismogram that differ from microseismic wiggles. Selection of UEO's requires a great deal of skill and experience in pattern recognition. The usual clues that a UEO has actually arrived are a sudden increase in amplitude or a change in frequency. The analyst will usually read the first onset of the wave correct to the nearest tenth of a second. Often, the amplitude and period of the wave are also read. If the onset of the wave is sharp, it is associated with the symbol "i" (for *impetus*), and if it is gradual, or emergent, it is associated with the symbol "e" (for *emersio*).

At some of the more advanced observatories, seismic signals from the seismographs are recorded on magnetic tape as a regular series of discrete numbers or samples. Such *digital* records pass directly into the memory of the digital computer. Since the availability of relatively inexpensive minicomputers with suitable memory capacity and speed, it has been feasible to have the minicomputer scan the recorded signal and flag UEO's according to pre-programmed clues. The computer then checks the accompanying time code and prints the arrival time of the onset. In this way some of the drudge work carried out previously by seismologists has become automated. However, in research work, when recalcitrant and esoteric UEO's are encountered, individual scrutiny of the records by a very experienced seismologist is needed.

The next step at the seismographic observatory is to try to identify the earthquake onsets and assign standard symbols (such as *P, S, PcP, SKS*, and so on). We will postpone the discussion of how the UEO codes are broken until the next section.

Finally, the arrival times, periods, and, if available, the identity of the onsets are then transmitted to other seismological centers. For example, many first-rank seismographic stations send daily readings of earthquakes or explosions by cable or airmail to the National Earthquake Information Service (NEIS) of the United States Geological Survey, in Golden, Colorado. These readings are used by NEIS to compute rapidly the locations and magnitudes of earthquakes around the world. Later, readings are listed in catalogs such as the complete one published by the International Seismological Centre in England.

Around 1960, observational seismology took its first leap forward since the pioneering instrumental developments of John Milne and others mentioned in Chapter 1. Largely as a consequence of the effort by several countries to find ways to discriminate between underground nuclear explosions and natural earthquakes, standardized improved seismographs were installed in many places around the world. This straightforward step transformed seismology from a neglected backyard in the physical sciences to a cultivated garden. The core of the upgrading was a network of about 120 stations distributed in 60 countries, called the World-Wide Standardized Seismograph Network (WWSSN). The instrumentation for the WWSSN, made available by the United States, consisted of six seismographs, one set of three short-period instruments and one set of three intermediate instruments. The peak magnification of the short-period instruments ranged between 3000 and 400,000 depending on the amplitudes of microseisms at the site; and magnification of the intermediate-period instruments ranged from 750 to 6000 (see Box 3.1). Crystal clocks and radio time signals were used to improve greatly the time-keeping. Recording was on photographic paper and seismograms were copied and placed in a library in the United States, accessible to any seismologist in the world.

Although some countries such as the USSR, France, and Canada did not participate fully in WWSSN, they also modernized their earthquake observatories and by the mid-sixties a standardized observational system for recording earthquakes was established. Naturally enough, vital fresh knowledge soon flowed from these observatory accomplishments; results involved UEO encounters of all kinds and much new light was shed on the fine structure inside the Earth. Many WWSSN stations are still in operation, and the records continue to be the backbone of the exploration of the Earth's deep interior. We are now in a period of renewed upgrading of observational seismology with stations operated by many countries being equipped with more flexible hi-fi, digital instrumentation. Some of the puzzles, uncertainties, and controversies that we leave dangling at the end of this book may be resolved with this equipment.

Another modern development is the installation of special seismographs to record very long-period surface waves and resonant vibrations of the Earth out to periods of almost one hour. These ultra-long period instruments are now on

Box 3.1   Magnification Curves for Seismographs

The magnification of a seismograph depends upon the period of the wave recorded. The response curves below are for photographically recording seismographs at Jamestown (JAS) and Berkeley (BKS), California. The Benioff and Sprengnether 15–100 second instruments have magnifications like the standard seismographs of the WWSSN system. The numbers refer to the resonant periods of the pendulums.

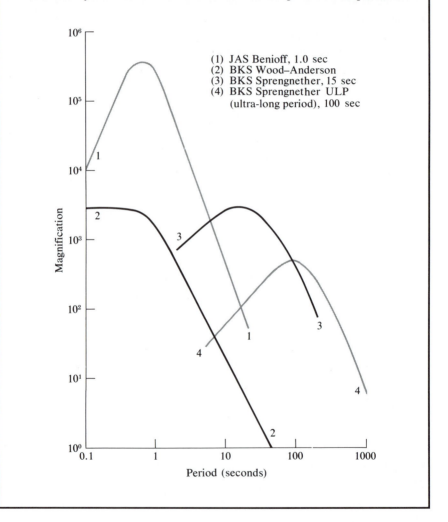

(1) JAS Benioff, 1.0 sec
(2) BKS Wood–Anderson
(3) BKS Sprengnether, 15 sec
(4) BKS Sprengnether ULP
    (ultra-long period), 100 sec

watch for large earthquakes at over twenty observatories around the world. As an illustration, one very recent important development has been the worldwide deployment of ten special instruments to record fluctuation in the Earth's gravity during earthquakes. This international digital array, dubbed IDA (International Deployment of Accelerometers), is already proving most effective in measuring the spectrum of eigenvibrations of the planet; we will touch on these vibrations further in Chapter 6.

To increase the capability to detect faint signals in the midst of microseisms, in the last twenty years seismograph *arrays* have been constructed (see Figure 3.3) by a number of countries. These arrays resemble in design and intention the radio telescope arrays set up by astronomers to detect faint radio signals from distant sources in the Universe. Wave detectors, spread out over a large area in a geometrical pattern, are linked to a central recorder so that the seismic waves can be recorded simultaneously.

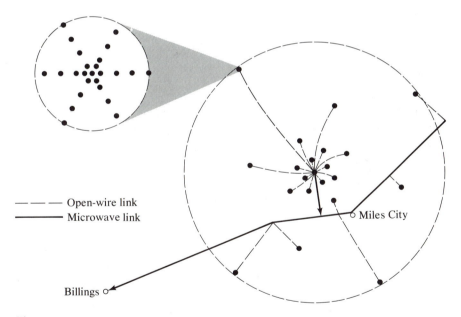

——— Open-wire link
——— Microwave link

Miles City

Billings

Figure 3.3 Large-aperture seismic array (LASA) installed near Billings, Montana, in the mid-1960's by the Department of Defense. LASA consists of 525 linked seismometers grouped in 21 clusters. In each cluster 25 seismometers are arranged as shown at the upper left. The array covers an area 200 km in diameter. [From Bruce A. Bolt, "The Fine Structure of the Earth's Interior." Copyright © 1973 by Scientific American, Inc. All rights reserved.]

Having such a spread-out seismograph has three great advantages. First, only one clock is needed so that timing errors between stations are eliminated. Second, because the microseismic waves arrive with more or less random phases from various directions, their amplitudes can be reduced relative to the earthquake waves by adding together the signals from all the wave detectors to produce just one seismogram. Third, by watching the front of a seismic wave as it travels across the array, a direction and speed can be assigned to the wave. This effectively discriminates the wave from other seismic waves that travel at different speeds and greatly enhances our ability to identify a UEO. As we will see in later sections, these advantages have led to important discoveries on Earth's structure.

One giant seismic array that provided particularly valuable results (referred to in Chapter 5) was the large-aperture seismic array (LASA) located near Billings, Montana (Figure 3.3). It was constructed in the 1960's but, sad to say, closed down in 1979. In 1980 there remain only about five large seismic arrays recording around the world, a decrease in number from the peak of twenty in the early 1970's.

Encountering UEO's on Seismograms

The seismogram is a doorway. At my desk with a seismogram spread out, I turn into an excited tourist, seeking a world as perplexing and foreign as the lunar landscape. Down there, within the Earth, undulating surfaces separate exotic rocks and, tantalizingly remote, the Earth's dynamo coils and intertwines. From experience, I have learned how to interpret many (but not all!) of the wiggly lines on seismograms in terms of such deep structures. But the nonspecialist who wishes to follow the evidence is definitely not precluded from understanding earthquake records. Curiosity is the only prerequisite to success, and clues to the innermost parts of the planet from pictures of the wiggly waves can now be explained. Box 3.2 provides the key.

To reassure the doubtful, consider some other, more familiar wiggly lines used nowadays to provide important information. For example, cardiographs produce wavy lines that are interpreted by doctors in terms of the rhythms of the patient's heart. Encephalograms, also displayed as continuous wavy curves, are used to monitor the activity of the brain. Specialists in these medical fields are able to infer from the recorded patterns of wave motions something about the condition of the patient (an example of a medical "inverse problem").

Fortunately, the interpretation of seismograms is more straightforward and firmly based than that of either cardiograms or encephalograms. This is because

Box 3.2 Travel-Time Curves for a Surface Source

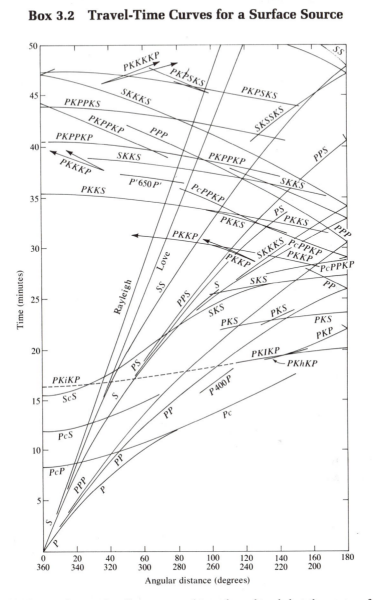

In this figure, the angular distances are the angles subtended at the center of the Earth by the radii to the epicenter and seismograph station. From the curve for *SS*, say, the time for *SS* waves to travel from Borneo to Berkeley (see Figure 3.4), a distance of 102°, is 32 min 45 sec.

[Based largely on the tables of H. Jeffreys and K. E. Bullen, British Association for the Advancement of Science, 1958.]

the recorded seismic waves are predicted by the physical theory of the passage of waves through an elastic sphere. As we mentioned in Chapter 1, this identification between theory and observation was first made by R. D. Oldham in 1897. The theory provides as aids the well-known laws of reflection and refraction, diffraction and scattering. With due allowances, seismologists can boast that if the structure of the Earth's interior was known, then, from elastic wave theory alone the arrival times and appearances of the various seismic waves could be computed and hence a predicted seismogram drawn.

Although such precise knowledge is not available, we are greatly helped by having empirical travel-time tables for the various seismic phases (*P, S, PcP, PKP,* etc.) often in the form of simple charts (see Box 3.2). These charts predict within a few seconds when the main types of seismic waves should arrive at a recording station, as long as the distance between the station and the earthquake source is approximately known. From such charts that predict transit times we can follow the progress of the various seismic waves throughout our planet (see Figure 3.5). As well, in recent years, "synthetic" seismograms have been calculated for a number of postulated Earth structures, and comparison with observed seismograms has shown the differences in the best cases to be small. But because we do not initially know the deep structure, we must always return from calculations based on postulates to the observations themselves.

Let us now make a step-by-step tour of a seismogram actually recorded at the Berkeley Seismographic Station in California. The record, given in Figure 3.4, was made by a long-period instrument. It shows the vertical ground motion at Berkeley from the shallow-focus earthquake that occurred near Borneo at an epicentral distance from Berkeley of 102° (about 11,000 km). The earthquake, magnitude 6.8, occurred at $12^h 41^m 36^s$ Universal Time on March 27, 1969. The seismogram was recorded on a paper sheet wrapped around a rotating drum so that the trace we see is a continuous spiral with time increasing from left to right. To view the complete seismogram clearly, the paper must be unwrapped and laid flat. Note that the time is shown by small upward offsets. On this seismogram, the time offsets are 1 minute apart, and there is a row of broader offsets that mark the hours exactly.

At first sight, we are struck by the large number of UEO's that have been recorded. As seismological detectives, we must now make use of the clues discussed earlier on the types of waves that can propagate through the Earth and of the laws of reflection and refraction.

The first encounter, marked with an arrow, is the first preliminary tremor *P* and occurs as a pulse that is bigger than the background microseisms at about $12^h 55^m 35^s$. This is the direct wave from the earthquake focus to Berkeley and

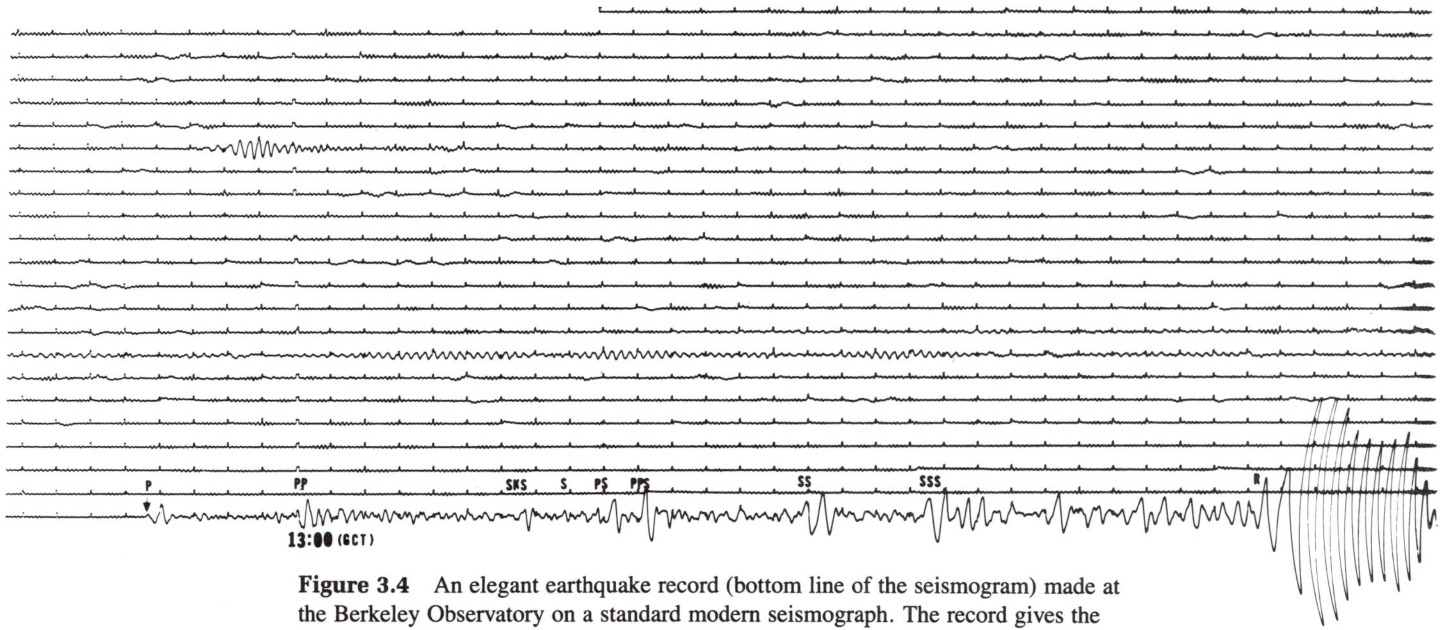

Figure 3.4 An elegant earthquake record (bottom line of the seismogram) made at the Berkeley Observatory on a standard modern seismograph. The record gives the vertical motion of the ground surface. The interval between the tick marks on the record corresponds to 1 minute, and time increases from left to right. This earthquake occurred near Borneo at a distance of 11,000 km from Berkeley. The onset of *P* waves is clearly seen, together with the *PP* reflection. This is followed by the onset of *SKS* and *S* waves and the reflections *PS*, *PPS*, *SS*, and *SSS*. At the end of the bottom trace can be seen the Rayleigh wave train, starting with long but decreasing periods (an example of wave dispersion). The record is not complete because the wave motion was interrupted by the operator inadvertently changing the seismogram.

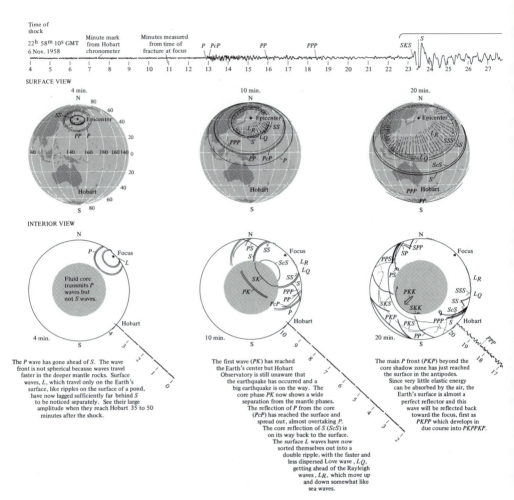

Figure 3.5 "Snapshots" of seismic waves of various types (marked on the seismogram at the top) at successive times as they move out from an earthquake near Japan through the body of the Earth (body waves of various *P* and *S* types) and across the surface of the Earth (surface waves). The reader can follow the wave fronts as they progress outward by looking at the seismogram recorded at Hobart, Tasmania. The lower diagrams show the wave fronts within the Earth at snapshots taken at 4 minutes, 10 minutes, 20 minutes, 40 minutes, and 50 minutes after the origin of the earthquake. [Based on a chart developed by Professor S. W. Carey, University of Tasmania.]

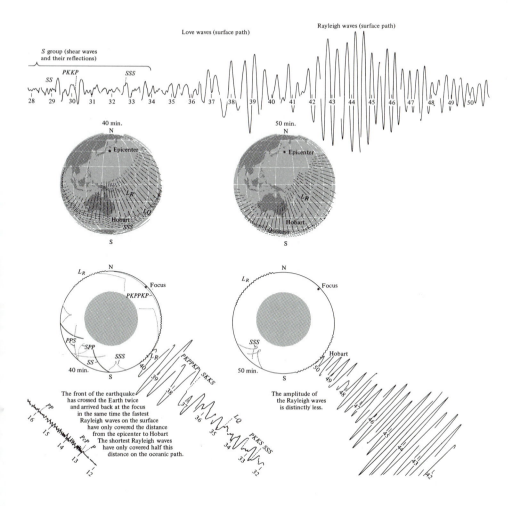

S group (shear waves and their reflections)

SS PKKP SSS

Love waves (surface path)

Rayleigh waves (surface path)

40 min.
N
Epicenter
L_R
L_Q
Hobart
SSS
S

50 min.
N
Epicenter
L_R
L_Q
Hobart
S

L_R N Focus
PKPPKP
PPS SPP SSS L_R
SS
40 min.
S

L_R N Focus
SSS
Hobart
50 min.
S

The front of the earthquake has crossed the Earth twice and arrived back at the focus in the same time the fastest Rayleigh waves on the surface have only covered the distance from the epicenter to Hobart The shortest Rayleigh waves have only covered half this distance on the oceanic path.

The amplitude of the Rayleigh waves is distinctly less.

PKPPKP SKKS L_Q PKKS SSS

PP PcP P

has taken about 14 minutes to complete the passage. The next strong UEO hits about $4\frac{1}{2}$ minutes later and has been identified as *PP*. This is the ray that is once reflected at the outer surface between Berkeley and Borneo (see Figure 2.3). Then, ignoring the minor wiggles on the seismogram, the next main onset is the pulse tagged as *SKS*, which comes through the Earth's core. This is followed by the wave onsets marked *S, PS, PPS, SS* (a large and clear onset with long period), and *SSS*. The ray paths through the Earth of these phases can be easily drawn as in Figure 2.3.

Finally, 32 minutes after the *P* onset, an elegant train of waves begins—these are surface waves that come across the Pacific Ocean and pass by Berkeley for another 30 minutes (the end of the record is not shown). Incidentally, some wave dispersion can be seen in this train with the long-period waves arriving first. Are these Love or Rayleigh waves? Well, there can be no Love waves on this record because, as Love motions are parallel to the Earth's surface, they are not recorded by a seismograph that responds only to vertical movements. Rayleigh waves do shake the ground vertically (see Figure 2.4), so we identify the surface waves in Figure 3.4 as Rayleigh waves.

This moderately sized earthquake illustrates how a pattern, rich in information, is built up by waves that radiate out from the earthquake source. Not all records have onsets that flaunt themselves along the seismogram like those of Figure 3.4. We can conjure up many difficulties. For example, a body wave might be reflected inside the Earth so many times that it would take more than 30 minutes to travel to Berkeley and would thus arrive along with the surface waves and be obscured. Here we see another advantage of using as probes deep-focus earthquakes, which have almost no surface waves, rather than shallow ones, which do. Because late phases rattle around inside the Earth, sometimes for about one hour after the first *P* arrival, deep-focus earthquakes produce seismograms that do not hide the arrival of these very delayed signals. We will display some cases of these late arrivals in Chapter 4.

As the climax of our description, let us now follow some seismic waves through the interior and around the surface of the Earth. We can do no better than use an elegant seismogram of a Japanese earthquake recorded at the Hobart Observatory, Tasmania. The record is displayed in Figure 3.5 along with snapshots showing where the fronts of the main seismic waves are at sequential times after the earthquake commences. The spreading wave fronts of *P* and *S* and their reflected families can be followed both on the surface and inside the Earth. As well, the Love and Rayleigh waves can be seen progressing around the Earth's surface.

Keith Edward Bullen (1906–1976)
"I have a debt to Nature for having arranged some interesting compressibility properties in the Earth, which enabled me to link my earlier work with notions about the solidity of the inner core."

CHAPTER 4

The Main Shells
of the Earth,
the Moon, and Mars

Crust

One of the earliest triumphs of seismology was the discovery that the Earth has a crust—the insight of A. Mohorovičić (see Chapter 1). He interpreted UEO's on seismograms from Balkan earthquakes as having traveled not only by direct paths through the top part of the Earth, but also along rays that had first traveled down and then been refracted along a boundary, now called the Moho, about 50 km beneath the surface before turning upward again to the seismographic station. (The relevant ray paths are shown in Box 2.1.) Subsequently, much work along the same lines using refracted waves has been done in various countries, and a picture of a worldwide continental crust ranging in thickness from 25 to 40 km has emerged. Similar seismological methods, using ships to deploy recording instruments at sea, followed later and showed that the crustal thickness under the deep ocean was much thinner, about 5 km. An immediate query might well be: given modern technology, is there not now much more direct evidence for a Moho? Let us answer this question.

In fact, the method used by Mohorovičić is one of two principal uses of seismic waves to probe crustal structure. (In later sections we will see that these methods carry over to probing the deep interior.) The second method uses waves *reflected* from the interior boundaries rather than *refracted* along them. Reflection seismology involves rather straightforward field techniques and interpretation schemes and is quite effective so long as the reflecting surface is an efficient one that sends back strong waves to the seismographs.

The most extensive use of reflection techniques using such artificial wave sources as explosions or mechanical ground shakers is in oil exploration. Discovery of oil and mineral deposits obviously needs a detailed knowledge of subsurface Earth structure, even though usually on a limited regional scale and to depths of only a few kilometers. Especially nowadays, with the Earth's resources being stretched to their limits, there is sharp worldwide demand for detailed mapping of geological structure.

During 1976, for example, the total expenditure worldwide on reflection seismology exceeded $1 billion, and most of this money went to petroleum exploration. As might be expected, such large-scale effort by the petroleum industry has led to the development of highly sophisticated field methods and analysis of the recorded data. Hand in hand, of course, has been the availability in recent years of large-memory, high-speed computers, with the result that modern crustal studies, using both reflection and refraction techniques, bear little resemblance to the simple refraction methods first employed by Mohorovičić and other seismologists using natural earthquake sources.

It is most appropriate here to go straight to the most recent and sophisticated application of the seismic reflection method to map structure of the continental rocks below the sedimentary veneer (up to 5 to 10 km thick) and of the crystalline basement rocks to depths of 40 km and even into the underlying mantle to depths of 50 km or so.

In 1968, a special field experiment was carried out by the Bureau of Mineral Resources, Geology and Geophysics in Australia specifically to try to record reflections of seismic waves from boundaries deep in the crust. The operators first set out on the surface rows of dozens of seismographic recorders (called *geophones* in the field-exploration context); they then produced seismic waves by detonating explosives in holes ("shot points") in the rock nearby. In order to "catch" deep reflections echoing back almost vertically, they allowed the recorders to run for up to 20 seconds. (For a crustal thickness of 30 km and an average P wave velocity of 6.0 km/sec in crustal rocks (a reasonable value), the down-and-back time for a P-wave reflection from the Moho is about 10 seconds.) The whole operation would then be repeated farther along the traverse line. Figure 4.1 shows a fine example of the records obtained for a traverse near Mildura,

Figure 4.1   Reflections of seismic waves from explosions on the surface of the Earth recorded on a set of portable seismographs (geophones) set out across the surface. The vertical direction shows the pattern of underground structure as a function of time of reflection from discontinuities within the crust. Little structure is shown by the reflected waves before 10 seconds where a strong pattern clearly indicates a horizontal change.

Shot-points

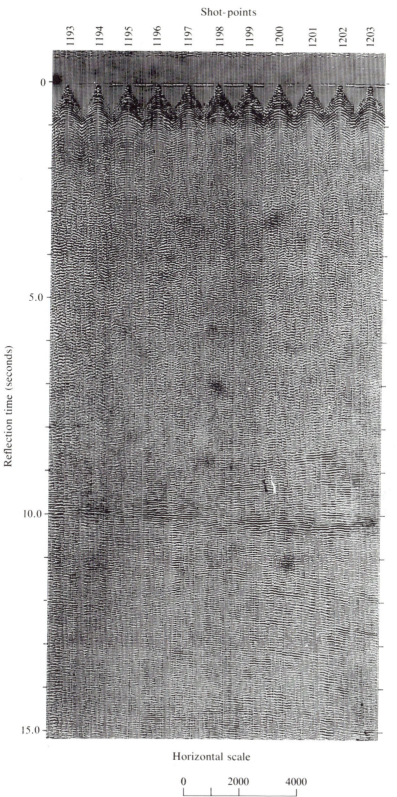

Horizontal scale

Victoria. The 12 km long profile of detonation points runs across the combined display while the travel time of the reflected *P* waves is plotted vertically.

The most striking detail on the record display is the almost horizontal pattern of darker lines (indicating incoming seismic energy) at a time near 10 seconds. From the above sample calculation, we can confidently assign these reflections to the Moho. This picture remains one of the best obtained of the foundation of the crust, although never published widely before. We might notice also that the reflecting layer, although not completely regular, extends only over less than half a second, indicating a layer of thickness of only about 1 km. Further, above and below this discontinuity few coherent patterns can be seen in the record display. We infer that in this part of southwest Australia the crust is rather homogeneous and is sharply separated from the mantle below at a depth of about 30 km.

In the early days, seismological work gave an impression that became surprisingly widespread among geologists (who after all grapple with complicated surface structures) that the crust everywhere had a bland and simple architecture. Only recently is the question being faced: just what is the structural fabric of crustal rocks? To answer, we turn to another recent productive technique using reflections called VIBROSEIS, developed by the Continental Oil Company. Instead of an impulse generator at the surface, such as an explosion or a weight drop, a vibration mechanism mounted on a truck and driven by a large motor serves as the source of the seismic wave energy. The vibrators impart vertical forces up to about 30 tons over a 2 square meter area of the ground surface. The force produced is approximately like a sine wave in time, but it has a slowly varying frequency. The durations of the vibrations are usually about 20 seconds, and the frequency is varied in a linear way from about 8 to 32 Hz during this interval. The reflected signals are recorded on magnetic tape from an array of many seismometers set out in a profile across the ground. These recorded signals are then correlated with the input signals.

The method has many advantages, including elimination of drilling holes for explosives, efficient coupling of the source energy into the seismic waves, and more precise control of the characteristics of the source of the waves. In some successful experiments, the seismographs in the field were spaced at intervals of about 100 m, and 100 stations were established along a profile 10 km long. At each one of the stations, a mini-array or "spread" of about 30 geophones was deployed to discriminate between natural and source noise by summing all the signals (see Chapter 3 on arrays).

The spectacular result of one experiment is shown in Figure 4.2. This work was carried out in 1976 and 1977 along the Wind River uplift in the Wind River

Mountains, Wyoming, by a group from the Department of Geological Sciences at Cornell University in New York. As in Figure 4.1, the picture of the side elevation of the Earth's crust is displayed after computer processing, as a function of the two-way travel time of the seismic *P* waves downward from the VIBROSEIS vibrator and upward to the surface again. As in the Mildura picture, multiply by 3 to convert the time roughly to depth in kilometers.

If we move from southwest (left) to northeast (right), we first see in the Green River Basin reflections from numerous layers in the sedimentary veneer. These sedimentary rocks attain a maximum thickness of 12 km along this section and are gently folded. As we move toward the Wind River Mountains, we see steeply dipping reflectors that define thrust planes that plunge downward into the crust (see arrow from B to D in Figure 4.2). This agrees with surface geological

Figure 4.2   A seismic reflection "X-ray" of the Earth's crust in the Wind River Mountains, Wyoming. As in Figure 4.1, the horizontal scale represents a distance on the surface of the Earth, and the vertical scale represents the two-way travel time of the waves downward to a reflecting layer and back to the surface. You can see a considerable amount of structure that has reflected *P*-wave energy back to the surface after being generated there. The structure has been associated with the Wind River Uplift and the Green River Basin.

evidence that sedimentary rocks in the Green River Basin have been overturned by Pre-Cambrian rocks of the Wind River Mountains. The seismic display also shows deformation by folding and faulting of the sedimentary rocks under the thrust (at C and A). The thrust plane continues between the crystalline basement and the sediments to about 3.8 seconds (i.e., 12 km depth), where the sedimentary layer terminates. A continuation of the profile, not reproduced in Figure 4.2, demonstrates, however, that the thrust plane goes past this sedimentary basin and continues to a time of 9 seconds, corresponding to a depth of about 25 km.

The reflection patterns in Figure 4.2 in other parts of the Wyoming crust show a good deal of variation, which we shall not describe here in detail. While the upper crust in the mountains does not show many reflectors, the middle crust shows numerous reflecting horizons, indicating a contorted rocky fabric. The whole display gives us a bird's-eye-view of the heterogeneous and complex nature of the crust of the Earth as though we could cut away the crust and look at it directly.

We must also beware, of course, that just as "beauty is in the eye of the beholder," so sometimes a perceived pattern might be the fulfillment of a personal expectation. Perhaps there are some places, for example, where there are unclear gradations between crustal rocks and those below.

Mantle

A simple way of naming the different major shells of the Earth's interior is helpful. In Table 4.1 we follow the scheme, first suggested by K. E. Bullen, of shells A through G, with slight changes for shells B and C to accommodate recent usage.

We have already probed shell A, which identifies the crustal layers. Now let us consider the Earth's mantle, which extends from the Moho to the mantle-core boundary. We have noted already that throughout this region both P and S waves propagate (apart from perhaps within local molten blobs) so that we are dealing with solid rock in the "ordinary" sense.

Detailed study of seismic waves has led to a subdivision of the mantle into further shells, although the divisions are not as precisely determined as the Moho. At the top there are two relatively thin, but unquestionably highly significant, shells called B and C. These layers appear to vary in thickness and physical properties from place to place, and seem intimately connected with the dynamic geological processes that cause the topographic relief and tectonic variations on

Table 4.1   Main shells of the Earth's interior.

Shell	Descriptive name	Range of depth (km)	Physical state
A	Crust	0–5 (oceans) 0–40 (continents)	Liquid Solid
B	Noncrustal lithosphere ⎫ Upper ⎬ mantle	Moho to 100 km	Solid
C	Asthenosphere ⎭	100–640	Solid (upper parts near melting)
D′	Lower mantle	640–2780	Solid
D″	Transition shell	2780–2885	Solid (lower velocities)
E	Outer core	2885–4590	Liquid
F	Transition shell	4590–5155	Liquid
G	Inner core	5155–6371	Solid

the surface of the globe. Indeed, to look at the matter in terms of global tectonics, the crust (shell A) is but the upper portion of a more or less rigid outermost shell called the *lithosphere*. The layer (shell C) just below this, which is marked by low seismic-wave velocities (first convincingly inferred by B. Gutenberg) and high seismic-wave attenuation, is called the *asthenosphere*.

It is convenient nowadays to identify shell B with that part of the lithosphere below the crust. The behavior of seismic rays indicates that the base of the lithosphere is not a very sharp or definite interface, although there is some seismological evidence, particularly from surface waves, that suggests a bottom depth of about 80 to 100 km. The asthenosphere upon which the lithosphere floats is designated shell C in Table 4.1. There is seismological evidence, however, that shell C contains at least two widely occurring layers with an interface at about 400 km depth. The offsets in the *P* travel times that correspond to this boundary were first spotted in the early days of seismology by Perry Byerly of the University of California, and despite many new interpretations and new observations this feature has remained. The base of shell C coincides with another boundary marked by various effects on seismic waves. Interestingly, the depth of 640 km is close to the depth of the deepest earthquake foci detected in seismically active zones (see Chapter 3).

Let us now consider some of the evidence for layer boundaries associated with shell C. In 1968, R. D. Adams of the Seismological Observatory in New Zealand, and a year later, E. R. Engdahl and E. A. Flinn in the United States independently

observed small waves that arrived on seismograms slightly earlier than the echoes
PKPPKP (or *P'P'* for short—see Chapter 2 and Figure 4.3). Ordinary waves of
P'P' type make the long journey from the focus of an earthquake to the other
side of the Earth and are reflected back to a station in the same hemisphere as the
earthquake, having passed through the core twice. The precursor waves were
interpreted as *P'P'* waves that did not quite reach the opposite surface of the
Earth, but were reflected back from a discontinuity in the upper mantle as shown
in Figure 4.3.

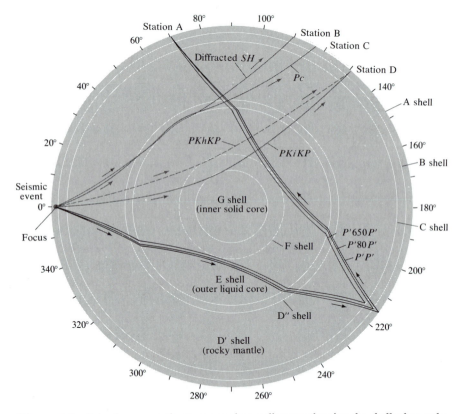

Figure 4.3   Seismic wave paths superposed on a diagram showing the shells that make
up the Earth's interior. The three nearly parallel rays arriving at Station A represent the
paths taken by seismic waves from a Soviet underground nuclear test whose
seismographic record is shown in Figure 4.4. The two rays arriving at Stations B and C
represent the paths of diffracted *SH* waves and *Pc* waves. *PKhKP* and *PKIKP* waves
reach Station D. [From Bruce A. Bolt, "The Fine Structure of the Earth's Interior."
Copyright © 1973 by Scientific American, Inc. All rights reserved.]

Waves of the $P'P'$ type are particularly useful for probing the Earth's structure. Their path is so long that they arrive some 40 minutes after they are first generated by an earthquake. Therefore, when they reach the seismograph, most of the other waves sent out by the earthquake have already arrived at the observatory and the instrument is quiescent.

A particularly striking example of multiple long-distance reflections was provided by an underground nuclear explosion at the Russian test site in Novaya Zemlya on October 14, 1970. The $P'P'$ waves passed through the Earth's core, were reflected under Antarctica, and returned to the northern hemisphere. In a recording made at Jamestown, the main echo $P'P'$ is the most prominent feature on the seismogram (see Figure 4.4). About 20 seconds before the onset of the large $P'P'$ reflections, a train of much smaller waves begins that can be explained as reflections from the underside of layers located in the 80 kilometers of rock below the surface of Antarctica. These forerunner waves are thus designated $P'80P'$.

As the eye scans the seismogram further from right to left (i.e. to *earlier* times), only inconsequential microseisms are seen for more than a minute and a half. All at once, almost precisely 2 minutes *before* the first $P'80P'$ waves, a beautiful doublet can be seen: two sharp peaks, separated by a few seconds, that

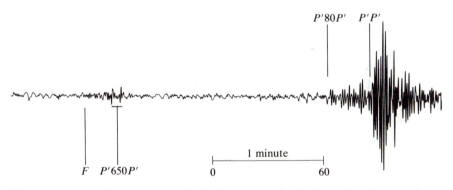

Figure 4.4   Seismic trace received at the Jamestown Station from the underground nuclear test on October 14, 1970, on the Russian island of Novaya Zemlya. The large phase $P'P'$ was produced by a compressional wave reflected from the other side of the globe under Antarctica (Figure 4.3). It was preceded by echo $P'80P'$, evidently reflected from a structure 80 km below the surface of Antarctica. Two minutes earlier still, the record shows doublet $P'650P'$, evidently reflected from a layer 650 km below the surface of Antarctica. The origin of the wave train starting at F is unknown. [From Bruce A. Bolt, "The Fine Structure of the Earth's Interior. Copyright © 1973 by Scientific American, Inc. All rights reserved.]

stand out clearly above the background shaking. These sharp pulses agree nicely with the expected travel time of rays reflected by a layer located some 650 km below the surface of Antarctica; hence they are designated $P'650P'$. The presence of a doublet means that there was a slight variation in the paths of the two rays reflected from the 650 km layer. This variation is presumably related to the transition layers of the core that we will discuss in Chapter 5.

Many other examples have now been reported of $P'P'$ waves arriving earlier than one would expect if the upper mantle of the Earth were uniformly smooth. The most straightforward assumption is that these precursor waves indicate the existence of rather sharp boundaries above depths of 640 km and that these boundaries probably are intermittent but worldwide features.

We should note, however, that the particularly clear seismographic record of the Novaya Zemlya test explosion shows no spikes between the $P'650P'$ waves and the $P'80P'$ waves, as we would expect if there were a sharp reflecting surface at some intermediate depth, such as 400 km. The absence of intermediate UEO's indicates either that perhaps such intermediate discontinuities are not present under Antarctica or that perhaps they are not so easily detected by short-period P waves that pass steeply upward because the shallower discontinuities are less sharp than the one at 650 km.

The fabric of the mantle below shell C is much blander. P and S waves move through the gigantic D shell with little complication and only a small amount of attenuation (see Figure 6.7). The speeds of the seismic waves change, on the average, smoothly and gradually as exemplified by the velocity curves in Figure 7.6. Nevertheless, somewhat muted and in the background, there are investigations that, by pushing seismological "X-ray techniques" to the limit, suggest variations in structure from place to place in the D shell. Compared with the sharp changes at the Moho and mantle-core boundary, and even at the 400 km and 640 km depth discontinuities, we could typify these gradations and textures as "second-order" changes in composition and elastic properties.

If we follow a family of P rays that bottom at deeper and deeper depths in the mantle, like those drawn in Figure 4.7, behavior is regular until we approach epicentral distances of about 105°. At about this distance, as noted by the pioneers such as Oldham, the amplitudes of short-period P-wave onsets on the seismograms begin to diminish more rapidly than previously so that beyond 105° the short-period P waves fade into the microseisms. A similar effect occurs with short-period S waves, although it is not as easy to observe as with the first-arriving P waves because the S onsets are somewhat obscured by other waves at these distances (see Chapter 5). Beyond 105°, additional odd behavior of P waves is encountered: the slope of the travel-time curve of the weak P waves becomes straighter and the energy in the P waves shifts to longer wavelengths.

For such reasons, the prevailing inference, in agreement with Oldham, is that the rays have encountered the distinct surface of a great obstacle, which creates a seismic shadow on the other side of the terrestrial globe. On this hypothesis, seismographic stations at distances beyond 105° are in a twilight zone, illuminated dimly only by earthquake energy that diffracts around the core or slips in along indirect or scattered rays.

It should not be overlooked in debates with skeptics that, apart from the above arguments, there is much more direct evidence for a sharp boundary at the base of the mantle. This comes from the reflections *PcP* and *ScS* (see Figures 1.3 and 5.3) that are commonly recorded from earthquakes at many epicentral distances and that point firmly to a surface at about 2885 km depth that can reflect *P* and *S* waves with wavelengths as small as 5 km.

There are, however, slight complications observed in the arrival times and amplitudes of *P* and *S* waves at distances near 100° which require some additional explanations. Perhaps the most successful inference is that there is a thin transition shell just above the core boundary (see Figure 4.3). For this reason the massive D shell is subdivided into D′ and D″ shells with the latter only 100 km or so thick. In the next chapter we will explore the D″ shell a little further, because it turns out, despite its small dimension, to have considerable implications to theories of convection of the rocks throughout the whole of the mantle and to temperature estimates in the Earth (see Chapter 7). In models in which the mantle turns over by slow convection, D″ is the stagnant layer at the bottom of the terrestrial "saucepan" through which heat conducts strongly from the core "hot plate" below.

Outer Core

In our voyage to the center, we have now reached shell E, which constitutes the enormous liquid outer core of the Earth. Of its liquidity, first established convincingly by Sir Harold Jeffreys of Cambridge University, there can be little doubt even with the cautions imposed by inverse problems (see Chapter 1). Tidal deformations due to the Sun and Moon observed for the whole Earth require a large central shell with zero (or very near zero) rigidity. Also, the observed resonant tones of the Earth that we discuss in Chapter 6 require a liquid shell. Lastly, despite much observational search, no seismic waves that have passed as *S* waves through the E shell have been discovered on seismograms.

We also note that the liquidity of a significant part of the core is the centerstone of the modern explanation for the Earth's magnetic field. This view is that the magnetism is due to electric currents circulating within the Earth and generated in some way by hydrodynamical motions of conducting liquid in the core. (Of course, this theory depends upon the seismological evidence and cannot itself "prove" that shell E is liquid. But no plausible alternative has been thought of.)

P waves of all wavelengths do travel efficiently through the liquid core, and the most reliable evidence at present indicates that the *P*-wave velocity changes smoothly and steadily downward from the core-mantle boundary for at least 1700 km (see Figure 7.3). Further, there is experimental evidence that makes it crystal clear that the attenuation of *P* waves in shell E from damping is very small indeed. We need only to turn to some exotic *P*-wave echoes in E that have only recently been observed. Let us only consider two related ones, called *P4KP* and *P7KP* (see Chapter 2 for notation).

With the advent of sensitive seismographs and arrays at quiet sites, we can now detect very minute signals that have been trapped inside the core and internally reflected there many times before emerging and returning to the surface (see Figure 4.5). Reflected core waves like *P4KP* are among these. Although such multiple reflections had been predicted, I remember well my own thrill to scan along a seismogram made at Jamestown station in California of an explosion on Novaya Zemlya and there—Eureka!—at the travel time predicted for a *P7KP* wave was an unmistakable tiny pulse nestling in the valley of microseismic background noise (see Figure 4.6).

It is doubtful that we will ever see a natural earthquake generate such clear examples of *P4KP* or *P7KP* waves as shown in Figure 4.6. Sharp onsets can be seen from underground nuclear explosions because they release energy in a way that is simpler than the way energy is released in most earthquakes. (In the future, planned experiments using nuclear explosions, set off in favorable locations and designed to present no hazard to the human environment, should provide still more sensitive probes of the final detail of the interior of the planet.)

What conclusions can be drawn from records of *P4KP* and *P7KP* waves such as those in Figure 4.6? First, the onset of the waves is quite abrupt. This confirms that the mantle-core boundary is a sharp discontinuity, perhaps extending over no more than 2 kilometers. Second, the additional distance represented by the extra three legs in the *P7KP* wave only reduces its amplitude to a third of the amplitude of the *P4KP* wave. This small decrease implies that the liquid outer core transmits short-period *P* waves very efficiently indeed.

Finally, these observations throw some light on a controversy concerning the possible presence of "bumps," perhaps 500 kilometers from one side to the other, on the boundary between the mantle and the core. The existence of such bumps has been suggested by Raymond Hide of the British Meteorological Office and by others to explain the variations in the strength of the Earth's magnetic and

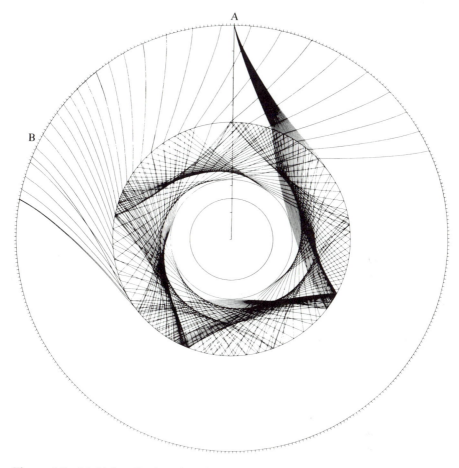

Figure 4.5 Multiple reflections from *P* waves trapped inside the Earth's liquid outer core. This computer plot depicts the paths of waves, generated by a seismic event at A, that have bounced inside the core seven times before reaching the surface, for example, at Station B. The computer program that produced the ray paths was devised by C. Chapman.

gravity fields as they are measured at different points on the Earth's surface. One way to detect such fine structure is to use short-period waves that interact with the boundary of the core. It can be calculated, however, that undulations on the mantle-core interface of less than 10 kilometers cannot easily be resolved with waves of the *PcP* type that return to the surface after a single reflection.

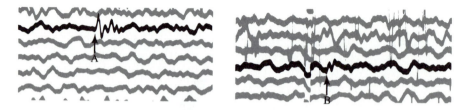

Figure 4.6   *P4KP* and *P7KP*. The faint pulse of a *P7KP* echo can be seen at the right (B) in this seismogram made at Jamestown of an underground explosion on Novaya Zemlya in 1970. The stronger *P4KP* pulse, labeled A at the left, was recorded about 20 minutes earlier. [From Bruce A. Bolt, "The Fine Structure of the Earth's Interior." Copyright © 1973 by Scientific American, Inc. All rights reserved.]

In contrast, if the multiple reflections *P4KP* and *P7KP* encountered topographic bumps on the mantle-core boundary more than 2 km high, the travel times of the waves would be altered enough for the variations to be measurable. By comparing the travel times of many multiply reflected waves at the same seismographic station, we should be able to derive the height of the bumps, if any, from the amount of variation in the times. Although studies of this kind are only a few years old, the present indications are that the variation is no greater than it is for waves that do not bounce from the core boundary. Therefore, I would tentatively say that if there are topographic undulations, either their height is less than a few kilometers or, if their height is significantly higher than that, they are few in number.

Inner Core

The inner core (shell G) was discovered in 1936 by Inge Lehmann of Denmark. The story is an attractive one. As has been told in Chapter 1, early seismological observations showed a shadow for *P*-wave arrivals beyond epicentral distances of 105° or so. Yet at the other side of the Earth, particularly at distances beyond 140°, unidentified earthquake onsets were seen stretching out to the antipodes at 180°. These UEO's were *P*-type waves, but delayed by 5 minutes beyond the times predicted from a simple extrapolation of the *P* travel-time curve for distances 0° to 105°.

A central core, as proposed by Oldham, with a sharp drop in seismic *P*-wave velocity at the boundary with the mantle explained these features closely. The rays that such a central core produces may be followed in Figure 4.7. A ray that

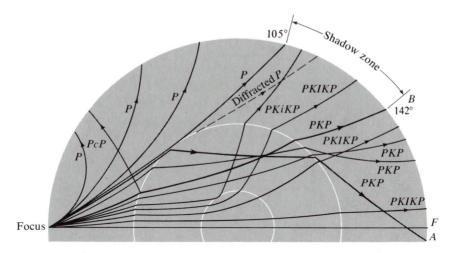

Figure 4.7 The paths of *P* waves through the Earth's core. The "shadow zone" between 105° and 142° is dimly illuminated by earthquake waves diffracted around the outer core and reflected and refracted from the inner core.

just grazes the core is refracted as *PKP* back to beyond 180° at point A. As the *PKP* rays become steeper, they refract back to shorter distances until at B, near 142°, they cease this backward progression. A wonderfully curious thing then happens, well-known by lens makers, astronomers, and opticians: the next steeper ray incident on the core boundary refracts out to a greater distance again. Indeed, steeper and steeper rays progress again in a normal way to greater and greater distances until at last there is a *PKIKP* ray that passes exactly along the diameter to the antipodes at F.

There is thus an illuminated cap on the other side of the Earth (from B to A) which is lit by the two types of *PKP* waves. The illuminated cap is bounded by a circle at 142° which is particularly bright. This circle is called a *caustic circle* and the point B a *caustic point*. The energy is greater at the caustic because waves reach it from both the inward and outward branches of *PKP,* so that the waves reinforce one another. (The effect of an optical caustic can easily be seen by viewing the bands of reflected light on the top of the liquid surface in a cup of tea, illuminated from the side; see Chapter 8, Question 27).

As mentioned in Chapter 1, the neat picture developed above became threatened in the 1920's when, with the aid of improved seismographs, observers spotted UEO's on seismograms in the gap between 105° and 142° that on the above core model (i.e., a unitary core) should be devoid of core waves. Various ideas were floated to account for these unexpected onsets, notably that such seismic energy was a diffraction pattern like the light fringe seen around an optical caustic produced by a spherical lens. Two decisive insights cleared up the problem once and for all. First, Lehmann showed that the whole pattern of observed *PKP* waves from 105° to 180° could be explained if the core consisted of two shells, an outer one around an inner core of radius smaller than that of the Moon (see Box 1.4). This radical notion was almost immediately endorsed by Beno Gutenberg, who by that time was working with Charles F. Richter at the California Institute of Technology, and independently by Harold Jeffreys, and they showed that the actual observations of travel times of core waves available to them fitted the double core hypothesis closely.

Second, what of the competing earlier diffraction hypothesis? This view was disposed of by a theoretical argument of Jeffreys, who demonstrated in 1939 that diffracted short-period (about 1 sec) *PKP* waves could be expected to be observed in a fringe to the B caustic back to no less than 135°; observed diffraction of *PKP* waves at distances from 110° to 135° was out of the question. Refracted rays that pass through the inner core, denoted *PKIKP,* are shown in Figure 4.7 passing into the shadow zone. It is these rays and the reflections *PKiKP* from the inner core boundary that pass into the shadow.

After the discovery of the inner core, the measured travel times could be transformed, using arguments of inverse theory (see Chapter 1 and Box 1.3) into plausible *P* velocities in the mantle and the outer and inner cores. In one of the most impressive and productive research programs ever carried through in the physical sciences, the two Cal Tech seismologists and Jeffreys (who worked at a crucial stage with K. E. Bullen) independently computed in the late 1930's average velocity distributions for the whole terrestrial interior based on thousands of observed travel times of *P* and *S* waves. Their agreement was impressively close. It is surely a great tribute that even after 40 years their solutions have not been much improved on. (For modern curves showing seismic velocities through the Earth, see Figures 7.3 and 7.6)

One item of initial but substantial disagreement, however, was the nature of the boundary to the inner core. In particular, Gutenberg argued that this interface was spread over many tens of kilometers depth, whereas Jeffreys felt that a sharp boundary occurred. The matter was left dangling until the 1960's when a search was made for definite observations of short-period reflections *PKiKP* from the boundary. About this time, I was working with Mary O'Neill at the University of California at Berkeley. If the inner core surface was sharp, a scrutiny of seismograms in the predicted time window at distances of 105–110° should disclose UEO's there. We looked and they were. Even more decisive evidence was supplied by the giant seismograph array LASA (Figure 3.3). In 1970, E. R. Engdahl, Edward A. Flinn, and Carl F. Romney in the United States announced that the Montana array had detected *PKiKP* echoes that had bounced steeply back from the boundary of the inner core at very short epicentral distances, only 10°. The sources of the echoes were underground nuclear test explosions in Nevada as well as earthquakes (see Figure 7.2). There were two immediate conclusions. First, the inner core has a sharp surface. Second, its radius is within a few kilometers of 1216 kilometers.

We cannot conclude the comments on the inner core in this chapter without speculating on an exotic core wave called *PKIIKP*. Its travel path is drawn in Figure 4.8; it has a single reflection on the *inside* of the inner core surface producing two *I* legs. After it became known in 1970 that the inner core boundary was a sharp interface from which short-period reflections *PKiKP* were commonly observed, it became possible to predict under what conditions an inner echo like *PKIIKP* might be detected by seismographic telescopes. While it was clear that

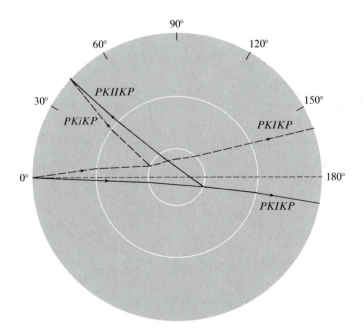

Figure 4.8 Rays corresponding to seismic waves traveling through the Earth's interior from a source at the point marked 0 and reflecting at the outside and inside of the inner core. These reflected waves are called *PKiKP* and *PKIIKP*, respectively.

it would be a very tiny wave, the resolving power of large seismographic arrays like LASA made a search for *PKIIKP* among all the UEO's and microseisms just worthwhile. This search, carried out independently by a number of seismologists, has turned up perhaps one observation that can be fairly confidently identified as *PKIIKP*.

A key step forward was the discovery by my colleague A. Qamar and me that the LASA array had clearly recorded, from the 1968 underground nuclear explosion in Nevada, code-named FAULTLESS, reflections from both the outer core (*PcP*) and the inner core (*PKiKP*). These observations are shown in Figure 7.2 and their implications are discussed in Chapter 7. The rays in this case travel very steeply down and back because LASA and the explosion are only a thousand kilometers apart. At once, however, the question arose whether LASA had also detected *PKIIKP* from FAULTLESS. I carefully searched the portion of the array recordings in the time interval when it might be expected. This unique seismogram is reproduced in Figure 4.9. (The time ticks on these traces are 1 second apart.) The top eight traces on Figure 4.9 span the time interval when *PKiKP* is expected to arrive and the bottom nine cover the predicted span for *PKIIKP*. Each trace corresponds to some special treatment of combinations of signals from subsets of seismometers of the array, but this filtering process need not concern us here.

The onset of a UEO is very clear on all top eight traces. From its time of arrival (and direction of travel known from the array measurements), we identify it as the bounce PKiKP from outside the sharp inner core boundary. Spotting a UEO on the bottom traces is more equivocal. Yet the arrow points to a short wiggle on the top three traces that falls within 2 seconds of the arrival time for *PKIIKP* that had been predicted some years before. It is also of interest that the seismologist who routinely scrutinized LASA seismograms on a daily basis had picked this wiggle as worthy of listing in 1968 without any thought for such rare waves as *PKIIKP*.

If the identification is accepted (the wave also has the correct direction of travel), then at least two important conclusions follow very simply. First, as Figure 4.8 makes obvious, if we subtract the time of travel down and back for the *PKiKP* echo from the corresponding travel time of *PKIIKP*, the difference is simply the time of travel along (approximately) double the diameter of the inner core. For a radius of 1216 km, this gives an average *P* velocity in the inner core of 11.14 km/sec. The second straightforward inference stems from the difference in amplitude and period of the recorded *PKiKP* and *PKIIKP* evident in Figure 4.9. A calculation based on these measurements indicates a very high rate of damping of the *P* waves in the inner core (see Figure 6.7).

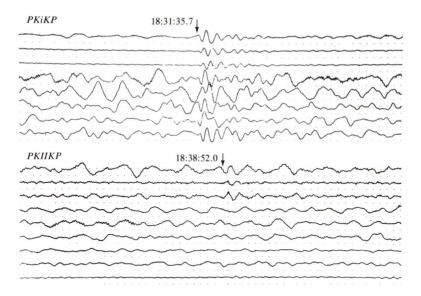

Figure 4.9   Seismograms of *PKiKP* and *PKIIKP* from the LASA seismic array in Montana. The time ticks are 1 second apart. The top three traces for both *PKiKP* and *PKIIKP* show the "beam" of LASA recorded signals that have been filtered at velocities and frequencies most appropriate for detecting a core wave. The remaining traces below are the seismic waves recorded by various smaller sets of seismometers. The arrows show the arrival times of the onsets of the *PKiKP* and *PKIIKP* waves in hours, minutes, and seconds.

Moonquakes and the Lunar Interior

From the beginning of planetary exploration scientists realized that a harvest of geophysical information could be reaped. Because seismology had already provided such a detailed picture of the structure of the Earth's depths, as well as vital information on interior constitution and tectonic forces, placement of seismographs on the planetary surfaces was given some priority. (Some geophysicists say not enough.)

Experiments to determine geophysical properties of the Moon were part of the U.S. and USSR space programs, starting with the early Ranger series in 1962. However, not until the Apollo landings were the first seismic probes landed on the lunar surface. By 1969, specially designed seismographs had been placed at five sites on the moon during the Apollo 12, 14, 15, 16, and 17 missions. Recording of seismic data ceased in September 1977.

The first exciting discovery achieved using the lunar seismographic stations was that there are, indeed, moonquakes. The stations detected between 600 and 3000 moonquakes every year of their operation, although most of the moonquakes were very small with magnitudes less than 2. A bonus for operation on the Moon is that the microseism background is very small compared with that of Earth so that quite high magnification can be used to operate the seismographs. Examples of recordings from moonquakes are shown in Figure 4.10. Their appearance is, at first, a shock because they reverberate much longer than seismograms from earthquakes of similar magnitude and distance. This long duration seems to arise from a high degree of scattering from fractured rocks in the upper part of the Moon and perhaps the absence of deep water, which damps seismic waves on Earth.

Because there was more than one station on the Moon, it was possible to use the arrival times of P and S waves at the lunar stations from the moonquakes to determine foci in the same way as is done on the Earth. However, as Figure 4.11 shows, the distribution of lunar seismograph stations was restricted to the front

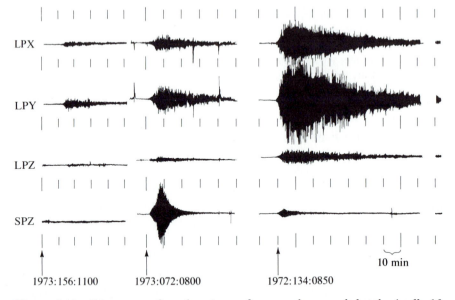

Figure 4.10   Seismograms from three types of moonquakes recorded at the Apollo 16 station. LPX, LPY, and LPZ are the three long-period components, and SPZ is the short-period vertical component. The first column shows a deep-focus moonquake; the center column, a shallow moonquake; the third column shows records of the impact of a meteoroid on the lunar surface. [Courtesy of NASA.]

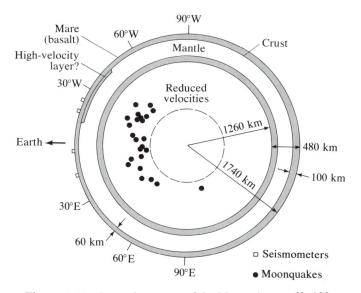

Figure 4.11   Internal structure of the Moon. A crust 60–100
km thick overlies a two-layered mantle with a transition zone
betwen 400 and 480 km. Foci of typically observed moonquakes
are shown. The inner region, within the dashed circle, shows a
sharp decrease in *P* and *S* wave velocities. [Courtesy of N. E.
Goins.]

of the Moon, giving considerable uncertainties in locations and travel times. A
consequence is some unsureness of structure and some frustration for seismologists working on the problem.

Moonquakes come in three kinds. First are the events caused by the impact of
objects, both man-made and natural, on the surface of the Moon. For example,
the third column in Figure 4.10 records the impact of a meteorite on the lunar
surface. A great many such recordings were made of meteoritic impacts even at
a range of 1000 km away from the stations. As well, pieces of the lunar spacecraft
were deliberately programmed to crash back on the lunar surface. These provided
artificial moonquake sources, which help with estimating the seismic-wave velocities within the Moon. Such crashes generated seismic waves strong enough to
produce clear seismograms, and because the impact point and time are known
precisely (unlike the foci of natural moonquakes), the travel times of the seismic
waves between source and receiver are known directly.

The second type of moonquake occurs at shallow depths down to 100 km.
These moonquakes are not very common and their locations do not show a

structured pattern on the lunar surface. The center column of Figure 4.10 exhibits recordings from such moonquakes. One explanation for them is sudden release of elastic strain in the rocks within the Moon's lithosphere, perhaps associated with fracturing around the great lunar basins.

The third type of moonquake was a surprise. These are relatively deep, with focal depths of 800 to 1000 km. The cause for the deeper lunar quakes is not known, since they do not seem to coincide with any major interior structural boundaries inferred from the travel times of the P and S waves (although this seeming disparity may be only an artifact of the imprecisions of this inverse problem). They appear localized at about 80 centers in the middle part of the Moon's interior. It is common to find that these deep moonquakes occur within a few days of *perigee,* i.e., when the Moon's orbit is closest to Earth. In other words, there is a periodicity related to the tidal pull of the Earth, and we may fancy a related triggering mechanism. An example of a seismogram from these deep moonquakes is given in the first column of Figure 4.10.

The Moon's radius, 1740 km, is about 40 percent greater than that of the inner core of the Earth. Its structure, as inferred from seismic travel times and paths of seismic rays, is quite different from that in the Earth. Investigators, following the tried and true methods developed for terrestrial exploration, have suggested an internal structure of the Moon like that in Figure 4.11. To a depth of 1000 km, it now appears to be fairly well understood. A lunar crust, less dense than the material under it, varies in thickness from 60 to 100 km. At the Apollo 12 site on the lunar highlands, the crustal thickness is about 60 km. Within the crust, there is a change at a depth of about 20 km, which appears to be the marker for the closure of cracks in the outermost rocks.

The lithosphere of the Moon extends from the surface to a depth of about 400 to 500 km, and within this lithosphere the seismic wave velocities are similar to those on Earth: 7.7 km/sec for P and 4.45 km/sec for S. Some workers surmise that there are negative velocity gradients within this shell and lateral heterogeneities are likely. As shown in Figure 4.11 there may be a transition zone between depths of 400 and 480 km. In any case, below 500 km the seismic wave velocities appear to decrease to depths of about 1000 km, which is the limit for deep moonquakes.

For a long time there has been speculation about the existence of a core, like that in the Earth, for the Moon. Unfortunately, the available seismic data give little information about the central region below 1000 km. P and S seismic waves are attentuated below these depths, and this behavior, together with the probable fall in velocities, is consistent with a softening of the rocks, and so with a liquid core in which the S velocities would drop to zero. If there is a liquid core, then the available recordings indicate that it is less than 350 km in radius.

Mars

A seismic probe has barely begun of the red planet. The landing of Viking 1 on July 20, 1976, and Viking 2 on September 3, 1976, placed the first seismographs on Mars.

Mars has a radius of 3385 km, about that of the Earth's central core. Its mean density is only 3.96 g/cm^3 or 20 percent greater than that of the Moon. Space probes detect no magnetic field so it is surmised that Mars has no convecting liquid central core. Pictures of the landscapes transmitted in the Viking missions show a desolate rocky surface with lavas eroded into ridges and troughs and drifts of sand (see Figure 4.12). Like the Earth in the pre-seismological age, the interior of the planet has been only a subject of speculation and "a playground for mathematicians." In the latter spirit, we can essay a plausible model for the interior based on analogy with Earth. Work that I did some years ago indicates, for example, a density increasing steadily from 3.28 at the surface to 5.33 g/cm^3 at the center. The interpretation is that the constituent material is mainly silicate rocks, like those in the upper mantle of the Earth, mixed with a small amount of iron. We eagerly await a time when such models can be tested against seismological information such as might be obtained in further Viking missions. Who can say if some day someone will be able to follow Oldham's footsteps and discover a definite nucleus to Mars?

Because of strict power and weight constraints on the Viking lander, the design of the seismograph package was restricted in 1976 to recording three components of ground motion at short periods. Furthermore, the sensors could not be placed on the Martian surface, but remained attached to the lander's frame.

Figure 4.12   Martian landscape at the Viking 1 lander site. This photograph was taken at 7:30 AM (local Mars time). The large boulder at left is 1 meter tall and is about 10 meters from the spacecraft. The boom in the center of the photograph is part of a miniature weather station. [Courtesy of NASA.]

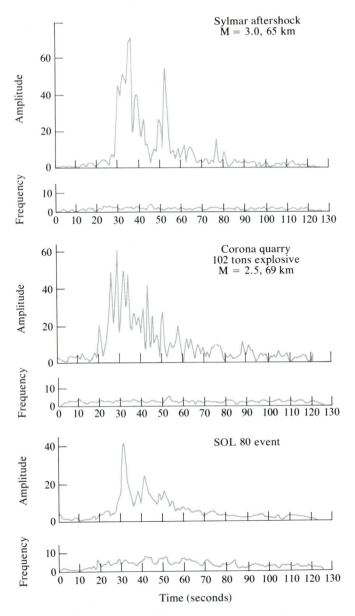

Figure 4.13 Comparison between amplitude and frequency variations (as time increases from left to right) of two terrestrial seismic events and a seismic event on Mars, called SOL 80. The SOL 80 event is similar to an aftershock of an earthquake sequence near Sylmar, California, and from a quarry blast at the Corona quarry, California, from 102 tons of explosives. The "marsquake" was recorded by a seismometer on the Viking spacecraft. The distance given is from the source to the seismometer, and *M* is the magnitude. [From D. L. Anderson, 1979.]

The Viking seismograph weighed 0.5 kg and included sensors, amplifiers, filters, and electronics designed to detect automatically seismic events and to store the data temporarily until transmission to Earth. Because of high accelerations during launch separation from the orbiter spacecraft and shocks at touchdown, the sensors require protection. For this purpose, spring-loaded plungers held the sensor masses firmly until released by fuse wires melted by electrical heating. Unfortunately, in Viking 1 the plungers did not disengage on command, but the seismograph on Viking 2 operated as planned for 546 Martian days.

Are there marsquakes? The aims of an experiment with a single seismograph were, of course, reconnaissance ones. It was feasible to try to measure microseisms, detect any local marsquakes and perhaps meteor impacts, and record large teleseismic marsquakes. However, vibrations caused by gusty winds blowing on the lander much hampered detection and identification of seismic onsets. After long forensic work, only one event (on Marsday 80) remained as a possible candidate as a marsquake.

In Figure 4.13, the amplitude and frequency of the recording of this event are compared with similar recordings of a natural earthquake and an explosion in California. According to Don Anderson of Cal Tech, who closely studied the Viking signals, the seismic signature "is unlike any definite wind-generated signal. It is the only signal that occurred during the normally quiet period of the early morning. The amplitude variations are similar to the California local events. If this event was, in fact, a natural marsquake, it had a magnitude of 3 and occurred 110 km from the lander." If this identification is correct, there would be a profound tectonic consequence, indicating, for example, great geological dissimilarities with the Moon. A moonquake of the above characteristics would generate a signal lasting hours on the moon instead of the 1 minute duration on Mars.

In summary, the Viking seismograph has not carried our knowledge of the Martian interior much forward. It has shown, however, that microseisms on Mars are relatively low so that a future seismograph placed on the ground, rather than the lander frame, could operate at high sensitivity. Second, it has indicated that marsquakes are not very common, but may occur from time to time. The door to X-raying Mars by seismic methods is still open.

Inge Lehmann (b. 1888)
The inner core is "a hypothesis which seems to hold some probability, although it cannot be proved from the data at hand."

CHAPTER 5

Finer Structural Detail

Lithosphere

There is a very simple way that earthquakes map Earth structure. We have seen it already in the map of world seismicity shown in Figure 3.1. These plots of thousands of epicenters indicate the surface regions where the tectonic action is. If we move to a three-dimensional picture by considering also focal depth of earthquakes, the plots of earthquake foci below the surface give some of the most crucial yet straightforward clues on structure and geological forces known to man.

A particularly arresting illustration of 3-D seismicity is reproduced in Figure 5.1. In this diagram we look sideways into a slice of the Earth running essentially east-west under the northeastern part of Honshu, Japan. To the east (right side) is the deep trench under the Pacific Ocean off Japan and to the west is the Japan Sea. The foci of many hundreds of recent earthquakes are plotted as circles. We see at once that many of the earthquakes have focal depths to 250 km, which places them far below the crust. These deeper foci mark out a zone that dips down beneath the ocean trench and underneath Honshu itself at an angle of about 30°. (The horizontal and vertical scales are not equal in Figure 5.1.)

The Honshu dipping zone is but one example of similar patterns of deep-focus earthquakes observed around the world at active island arcs. This pattern seems to have been first described as a global phenomenon by California seismologist Hugo Benioff in 1954. For this reason, the inclined zones of deep seismicity are

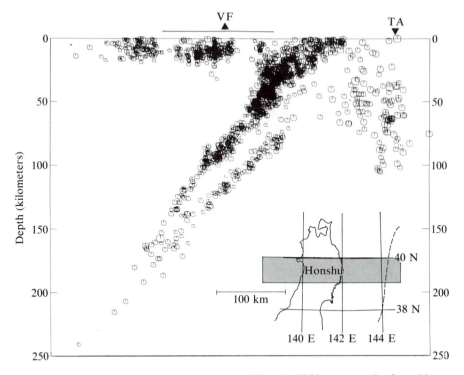

Figure 5.1   Foci of earthquakes recorded in 1975 and 1976 by a network of sensitive seismographs in Honshu, Japan. VF is the volcanic front; TA is the Japan Trench axis. The foci are drawn as a side elevation with depth in kilometers. The Benioff zone can be clearly seen dipping from the Japan Trench just west of TA toward the west. The deepest earthquake is at about 240 km. The striking feature of the Benioff zone is the two distinct lines of foci about 20 km apart that have been detected for this region. The seismicity plot also shows shallow earthquakes under Honshu within the crust as well as scattered earthquakes down to depths of 100 km to the east of the Japan Trench under the marker TA. [Courtesy of A. Hasegawa, M. Umino, and A. Takagi, 1978.]

now called Benioff zones. They dip under such regions as the South American Andes, the Tonga Islands, Samoa, the New Hebrides chain, the Japan island arc, Indonesia, and the Caribbean Antilles, each of which is associated with a deep ocean trench. Benioff zones commonly dip at an angle of about 45°, but some have shallower dips, whereas others have nearly vertical dips. On the average, the frequency of occurrence of earthquakes in the zones declines rapidly below a depth of 200 km, but some foci are as deep as 700 km.

The current explanation of Benioff zones is to identify the dipping zone with a slab of lithosphere that has bent at the ocean side of the deep trench and subsequently plunged down into the interior. The process is called *subduction* and is believed to be more or less continuous over long geological epochs, with the oceanic lithosphere slowly descending (at an average rate of a few centimeters per year) into the asthenosphere. Such a dynamic process would no doubt produce stresses all along the descending slab, and these localized stresses are believed to produce earthquakes. The most plausible model has the slab thickness about 80 km and has more rigid conditions (i.e. higher seismic velocities) within the slab than outside it.

In most Benioff zones, earthquake foci lie in a narrow layer 20 km thick near the top of the slab and are often identified with mechanical thrusting along or near the top surface of the slab. There is no universally accepted explanation, however, of why earthquakes occur in the pattern they do in the Benioff zones, and the puzzle has been recently made more cryptic by very precise studies like that illustrated in Figure 5.1. It is evident from this figure that the Benioff zone in Honshu is not a single but a *double* plane, unlike deep earthquake foci in some other parts of the world.

The Japanese study has a peculiar advantage—because there is a network of modern seismographs across northern Honshu, seismic waves passing upward from the foci can be read accurately and, by tracing rays between stations and foci, the focal positions can be precisely located. The locations fall in two thin layers, each approximately 20 km across and separated by an aseismic layer of similar thickness. This sandwich structure of Benioff zones has also been discovered in New Zealand, the Aleutians, and the Kuriles and has caused considerable excitement and speculation among seismologists and geologists.

Before leaving the subject of mapping inside the Earth using earthquake foci, let us shift attention for a moment to the best way of estimating focal depths in seismic zones that, unlike the Japan slab, are far removed from dense local seismographic networks. How do we know remote earthquake sources are deep? The answer hinges on the use of the handy seismic echo *pP* (or *sS* for the shear waves) that we sketched in Figure 2.2 and discussed in Chapter 2. As we stated there, the time lag between the *P* ray that travels directly to the distant surface station and the *pP* ray that first travels upward to the surface and then bounces back to the distant station is a sensitive measure of focal depth. In practice, the near-surface echoes *pP*, *sP*, *sS* are very often encountered clearly on seismograms. In Figure 5.3(b), very obvious near-surface reflections *sScS* follow the direct *ScS* waves and their multiples in a beautiful series of doublets and the two paths *ScS* and *sScS* are compared in Figure 5.3(a). Readers at seismographic observatories keep a vigilant watch for UEO's on seismograms that make up doublets because the second onset could well be the valuable *pP* or *sS* near-surface reflection from a deep earthquake. Once they are identified, the possession of focal depth is exposed and further calculation immediately gives the depth.

Not for the first time, as we question more deeply into earthquake probes we find a blemish on the elementary picture. The *pP* ray drawn in Figure 2.2 and the *sScS* ray drawn in Figure 5.3(a) are, of course, naively simple. The smooth paths of the rays drawn in these figures assume an Earth with perfect spherical symmetry. But, the perceptive reader will immediately inquire, what of the dipping Benioff zones and their interpretation as subducting lithospheric slabs? Such complex tectonic structures certainly violate simplistic assumptions of concentric structures that change with depth but do not change sideways.

Seismologists have met the challenge of the complicated slab by carefully tracing, from first principles, the appropriate seismic rays through and along the slabs in the same way an optician would trace light rays through a composite glass lens. Some results of considerable interest are just now forthcoming. In Figure 5.2, *pP* rays have been plotted by a computer (see Chapter 1) for an earthquake focus *F* at the middle of a dipping slab. The lens-like attributes of the slab with its difference in elastic refractive index from the surrounding rock are evident. For this particular geometry and elastic properties, *pP* rays that run up almost parallel to the slab are reflected sharply at the surface and, as a consequence, there is even a *shadow zone* produced. In this shadow zone, seismographic stations remote from the slab that are monitoring deep seismic activity would, in fact, be unable to detect *pP* onsets on the seismograms; the steady hum of the electric signals from the sensitive seismographs would give no warning double bleep.

By about 1970, the thickness of the Earth's crust appeared to be well determined. As we summarized in Chapter 4, the worldwide picture that emerged after the Second World War was of crustal rocks extending down to 5 km depth under the ocean floors and, in continental regions, varying in thickness between 25 to 40 km, or even more under some of the high mountains (see Figure 2.6).

More recently, however, new evidence has shown much deeper differences in structure beneath continents and oceans than provided by crustal variations. Indeed, such contrasts in structure may continue to depths of hundreds of kilometers and involve variation in rock properties extending below the lithosphere, of which the crust is only a part. We have already in Chapter 2 (see Figure 2.6) mentioned crustal roots under mountain chains; the suggestion here is of a thick lithosphere root underneath the continental regions. Using a dynamic analogy, the older continents, at least, would be like deep-hulled ships edging slowly through an ocean of viscous upper mantle rock. This point of view has been recently argued by T. H. Jordan, of the University of California in San Diego.

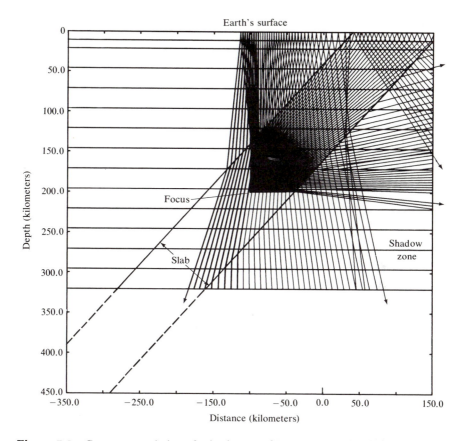

Figure 5.2   Computer rendering of seismic rays of *P* waves emerging from a focus of an earthquake situated deep within a dipping slab. The effect of the slab can be seen on the paths of the rays. The slab acts as a composite lens and refracts rays away from a simple pattern to a much more complicated one. Seismologically, the case shown corresponds to the upgoing waves *pP*, which are very important for the determination of the focal depth of earthquakes. [Courtesy of D. Michniuk.]

In his view, some of the best evidence comes particularly from rather unusual observations of prolific families of *ScS* waves. As shown in Figure 5.3(a), these shear waves travel nearly vertically downward from the earthquake source and are reflected from the sharp discontinuity between the solid mantle and the liquid core.

The importance of *ScS* as a seismic probe is that it is usually reflected from the core boundary with very little drop of energy. In the case of the horizontally polarized shear waves *SH*, no conversion to *P* reflected or refracted waves can

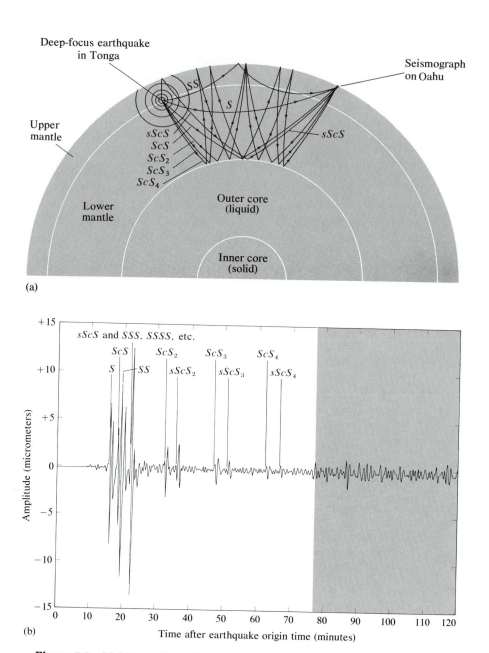

Figure 5.3 Multiple surface reflections (a) and seismogram (b) recorded at a seismographic station at Oahu, Hawaii. These waves followed a deep-focus earthquake near the South Pacific island of Tonga in October 1974. [From Thomas H. Jordan, "The Deep Structure of the Continents." Copyright © 1978 by Scientific American, Inc. All rights reserved.]

occur at the core boundary for reasons explained in Chapter 2. Thus, the ScS echo from the core that reaches the surface will be reflected once again downward, will again strike the mantle–core boundary, and again will be reflected upward with little loss of energy. The multiple surface reflections, ScS, ScS_1, ScS_2, ScS_3, ScS_4, are illustrated in Figure 5.3(a).

Jordan has found a most elegant seismogram showing a family of ScS reflections and it is reproduced in Figure 5.3(b). The record shows the horizontally polarized ScS waves on a seismogram at a seismographic station at Oahu, Hawaii, following a deep-focus earthquake near Tonga in the South Pacific in October 1974. The multiple echoes are marked as ScS_1, ScS_2 and so on. The last reflection from the Earth's core that can be seen is ScS_4, and it arrived about 64 minutes after the beginning of the earthquake. It is easy to see from Figure 5.3(a) that all these reflections have almost the same ray paths near to the source and station in the mantle. Thus, differences in travel times between the members of the family are probably a measure of structural differences near the surface reflection points. We should note that all the reflection points at the Earth's surface for this ScS family are under the Pacific Ocean between Tonga and Hawaii. Measurement of the times of travel of these multiply reflected ScS phases show that the average travel time of S waves moving vertically through the crust and lithosphere under the ocean basins is about 4 seconds greater than the travel times measured to other earthquakes to corresponding distances under the old continental shields. This delay is surprisingly large.

What does this sharp slowing down of the S waves under the ocean basins mean? One explanation is that zones of rocks with relatively low seismic velocities are more extensive under the oceans than underneath the continents. (This inference was independently drawn from seismological studies of surface waves over 20 years ago.) What is new is that, if a construction is attempted of oceanic and continental models that provide a 4 second delay for ScS, the anomalous zones need to extend down to at least 400 km. This type of seismic probe therefore gives an indication of a thick, strong lithosphere under the continents in contrast to a thinner lithosphere under the oceans riding on a less rigid (perhaps partially molten) zone. Of course, the ScS data do not prove that such a structure exists, and, as in all inverse problems, we can think of competing hypotheses.

We can map structure in the upper part of the Earth also by using the echo PP. Its path is shown in Figure 5.4. The idea is that any variations in the rocks at the point of reflection midway between the source and recording seismograph should show up by changes in wave properties. The simplest such property is travel time, and we might expect, for example, that PP waves penetrating through the crust to the surface would take longer than PP waves that reflect from the underside of some horizon in the lithosphere below the crust.

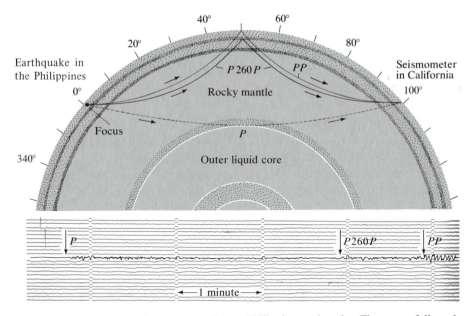

Figure 5.4   Waves and seismogram from a Philippine earthquake. The waves followed three distinct paths before arriving at Jamestown Station. In the seismogram the *P* wave arrived first, followed some 3 minutes later by the echo *P260P* that probably bounced off a reflecting surface 260 km deep in the Earth under the Pacific Ocean. The reflection from the underside of the ocean floor, *PP,* arrived another minute later. [From Bruce A. Bolt, "The Fine Structure of the Earth's Interior." Copyright © 1973 by Scientific American, Inc. All rights reserved.]

While this description is easy enough in principle, there are, as usual, a few clouds on the horizon. These are related to the fairly common difficulty in picking the true beginning of *PP* onsets on seismograms and to the difficulty in discriminating between structural variations under the reflection point and those near the earthquake source.

Let us consider first the observational situation. Examples of UEO's identified as *PP* onsets are given in Figure 3.4 and now in Figure 5.4. We note that in both cases the beginning of the *PP* pulse is not especially sharp (i.e., not *impetus*) and that some low-amplitude waves arrive about one minute before the onset marked *PP*. These tend to mask the beginning and make reading equivocal.

What are the unidentified waves that are seen just before the *PP* on the seismograms? Measurements indicate that the waves might have been reflected from the underside of layers located up to perhaps hundreds of kilometers below the Mohorovičić discontinuity. The waves arrive at seismographs as much as 150 seconds before the corresponding waves reflected from the underside of the Earth's surface.

As outlined in Chapter 2, we refer to these echoes generically as *PdP* waves, and a wave reflected from a layer 260 km below the surface is designated *P260P*. A clear example of such an echo is the UEO marked on Figure 5.4 that was produced by an earthquake on May 22, 1972, near the Philippines, and recorded at Jamestown. The distance between the focus of the earthquake and California is about 100°.

Such reflections do not always show up on seismograms but occur at scattered times and places. For this reason and others, some seismologists have suggested that the wave paths are not as symmetrical as drawn in Figure 5.4. Notwithstanding such reservations, many observations of *PdP* waves can be explained in terms of a roughness and lateral complexity of the rocky material in the upper part of the Earth's mantle that are capable of producing reflections.

Now let us consider a second use of *PP* probes. Because the origin time of earthquakes and particularly the focal depths are often only known imprecisely, a powerful procedure that minimizes this uncertainty is to subtract the time of arrival of the direct *P* wave from the time of arrival of the *PP* onset. Recently, a fascinating study was made using this method by Canadian seismologists I. C. F. Stewart and C. E. Keen. They used travel times of *PP* waves to detect an anomalous structure beneath the Fogo Sea Mounts in the northwest Atlantic Ocean. These sea mounts are enormous volcanic structures that rise 2 to 5 km above the level of the ocean floor and lie immediately south of the Grand Banks on line with Newfoundland. As shown in Figure 5.5 a strange blob was discovered by plotting the observed *PP* minus *P* times for *PP* reflection points along the profile AA'. There were very large delays for those rays that reflected in the vicinity of the sea mounts. Indeed, some of the delays exceeded 5 seconds even though, on the average, the time interval between *P* and *PP* on seismograms can be measured correctly to at least 1 second for reasonably sharp onsets. The *PP* wave delays, plotted in Figure 5.5 at the reflection points, map a 10° by 15° area in which the delays are always larger than those outside.

What is the reason for the variation? Perhaps these delays of the *PP* echoes are caused by variations of crustal structure or increased thickness of sediments which have low seismic velocities within the anomalous zone. There is, however, evidence to the contrary from reflection and refraction measurements made on oceanographic ships over the sea mounts. These data do not indicate sediments or anomalous oceanic crust. Another explanation, favored by the Canadian workers, is that there is a plug-shaped region with low seismic velocities present at this place in the upper mantle. It is tempting to speculate that this blob is a remnant

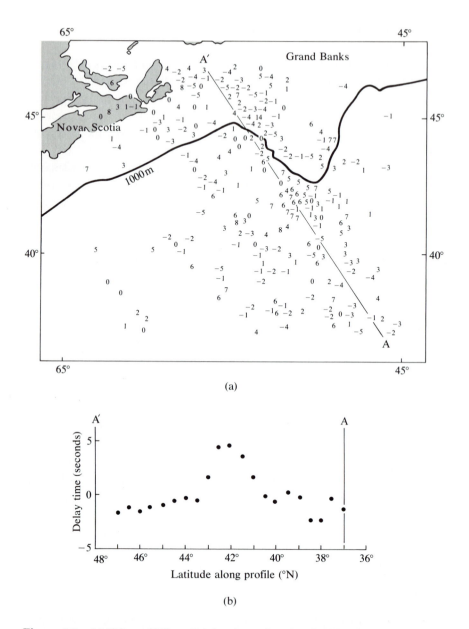

(a)

(b)

Figure 5.5 (a) Values of $PP - P$ delay times plotted at the PP reflection points and the location of profile AA′. (b) Values of averaged $PP - P$ delay times along profile AA′. [From I. C. F. Stewart and C. E. Keen, 1978. Reprinted by permission from *Nature,* vol. 274, no. 5673, pp. 788–791. Copyright © 1978 Macmillan Journals Limited.]

of a zone of partial melting 100 km or so deep that was associated with the volcanism that created the Fogo Sea Mounts 100 million years ago. Clearly, this type of earthquake probe is attractive because detailed structures beneath remote ocean floors can be explored by measuring seismic waves at regular earthquake observatories or simply looking up published catalogues of P and PP travel times.

Mantle–Core Transition Shells

The great rival research programs of Harold Jeffreys (sometimes in collaboration with K. E. Bullen) and Beno Gutenberg (often working with Charles Richter) in the 1930's laid bare the major interior structure of the Earth. These workers agreed that changes in the behavior of P and S velocities occurred near the base of the mantle. In a shell about 100 km thick around the core boundary the P and S speeds were, within the resolving power of the methods used, essentially constant. This shell, nowadays called D'' and shown as a stippled layer in Figures 4.3 and 5.4, has been given prominence in recent years. As was pointed out in the last chapter, the width and physical properties of this shell, despite its small extent, appear to be of vital importance in arguments on the temperature of the core (see Chapter 7) and the feasibility of gigantic convection cells rising from the bottom of the mantle to the lithosphere.

Before we sample some of the recent seismological evidence concerning D'', a warning is needed. There are at the present substantial differences of opinion concerning the seismic velocities in D''. Some seismologists hold that the speeds of P waves or S waves or both slightly decrease as the mantle–core boundary is approached. Some have inferred that the speeds stay almost constant, while others hold that there is evidence for horizontal changes through D'' with scale-lengths of tens and even many hundreds of kilometers. Indeed, there is much restlessness and volatility of attitude, rapid changes of assessment, and arguing at cross purposes. Basal heterogeneities with rising plumes of molten rock, massive scattering blobs, and mountainous anomalies appeal because they provide a kind of symmetry with the structural complexities and tectonics of the lithosphere. Yet such expectations must be tempered against the seismological evidence. A toxin of roughness in structure always creeps in when we use probes that have inevitably been affected by the considerable lateral changes in the lithosphere and crust.

With this warning in mind, we can still profit by taking a look at a few of the seismological methods that have thrown some light on the properties of the D'' shell. In the first place, modern observational techniques, unlike the simple use of the rather insensitive early seismographs (see Chapter 4), do detect unequivocally, small-amplitude waves of short-period *P* type at distances well beyond 105° in the shadow of the core. Such observations are surprising, because, as correctly postulated by Oldham, if the wave speeds remained constant or increased at the bottom of the mantle, the core would act as an opaque screen that would quickly cut off the direct, short-period seismic waves at about 105° (see Figures 1.3 and 5.4).

The actual situation can be compared to what happens when a shadow is cast on a wall by an opaque object illuminated by the sun. The shadow is not quite sharp because the light waves are diffracted, or bent, by the edge of the object. In the Earth some seismic waves get diffracted into the shadow produced by the Earth's core. Regardless of the actual velocity of *P* waves at the base of the mantle, therefore, the shadow region is always dimly illuminated with earthquake waves. It turns out, at least for some paths around the core boundary, that the strength of the short-period waves actually observed in the shadow of the core is greater than it theoretically should be if diffraction of the *P* waves in a shell of constant velocity were the only mechanism operating.

A few years ago I made a study of short-period waves designated *Pc* that have traveled out to more than 118° and have arrived at seismographic observatories in the core shadow zone with substantial strength (see Figure 5.6). The time of travel and the amplitudes of such waves indicate that they were refracted through the transition *D″* shell (see Figure 4.3) in a layer where the speed of propagation is perceptibly less than the speed that prevails only 100 km or so above the core boundary. A plausible calculation indicates that the *P*-wave velocity drops by a few percent in the *D″* shell above the Earth's core.

The evidence from the *Pc* waves does not stand alone. Let us shift our attention from *P* to *S* waves. Because the outer core is liquid, most kinds of *S* waves are inhibited from creeping around the core boundary as diffracted waves; their energy leaks off into the core in the form of longitudinal waves (i.e., to form *SKS* waves). There is, however, one type of shear wave, the horizontally polarized *SH* wave, that cannot produce *P* waves in the liquid core. As was noticed earlier, its energy gets trapped at the base of the mantle, and thus it can travel great distances. Very large *SH* pulses have been recorded at distances ranging from 90° to more than 150° from an earthquake (see Figure 5.7). From the measured travel times we can derive the velocity of the shear wave as it travels around the core boundary. Such calculations carried out in recent years by John Cleary of the Australian National University, by J. Mondt at Utrecht, by myself and colleagues working at Berkeley, and by others indicate that the *S*-wave velocity may decrease at the base of the mantle in the *D″* shell by 1 or 2 percent. As we have mentioned already, some workers using similar earthquake probes along different paths on

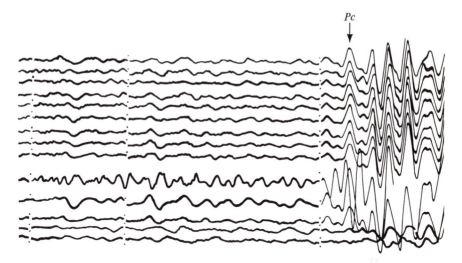

Figure 5.6 *Pc* waves from an earthquake in the South Sandwich Islands. The waves were guided with only small loss around the Earth's core by the D'' shell and were recorded at an angular distance of 118° by an array in Uinta Basin in Utah. Each wavy line was produced by a separate seismometer. Distance between breaks on the bottom line is 10 seconds. [From Bruce A. Bolt, "The Fine Structure of the Earth's Interior." Copyright © 1973 by Scientific American, Inc. All rights reserved.]

the surface of the core, and some using different types of probes, have found indications of a nearly constant velocity in D''. On balance, however, the evidence suggests slight sympathetic decreases in *P* and *S* wave speeds just above many sections of the core boundary. Perhaps, after all, it is safest to infer that the speeds vary from place to place in D'' due to lateral variations in properties. The idea is not a new one in the history of seismology. In his famous 1906 paper discussed in Chapter 1, R. D. Oldham commented on the variations in his measurements of seismograms:

> Another possible source of discrepancy is the possibility that the rate of propagation is not uniform in every direction, and that the time taken by wave-motion in traveling, say from Japan to Europe, is different from that taken by the same form of wave-motion in traveling from an equal distance in America. There are some indications that such is the case; but the difference is small, in comparison with the whole interval.

What do low velocities in shell D'' mean? One suggestion is that in this narrow shell temperatures rise rapidly toward the core (see Chapter 7) and the mantle

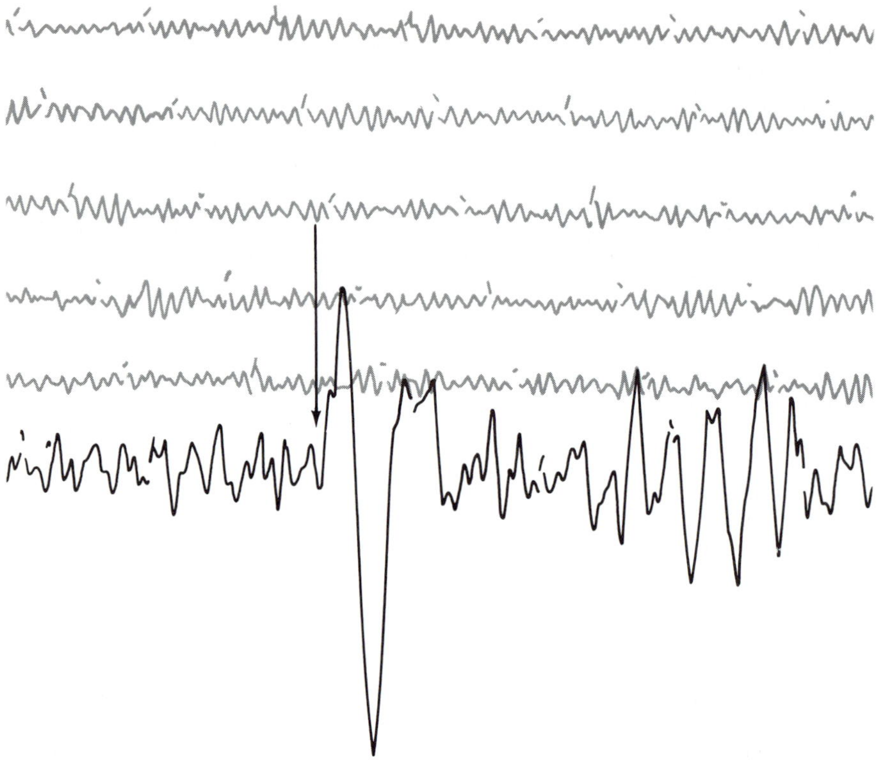

Figure 5.7 Horizontal shear wave, *SH,* produced by a major earthquake in Iran on August 31, 1968. The wave was recorded at a distance of nearly 108° by a seismograph at Berkeley, California, that responds only to horizontal ground motion. The large *SH* pulse sent the pen across the recording drum, crossing traces made earlier and later.

rocks become less rigid as they approach the core liquid. Another possibility is that the rock composition changes slightly in the D″ shell. Below the mantle–core boundary the measured physical properties indicate a material that consists mainly of iron. Perhaps there is about 10 percent more iron in the D″ shell than there is in the rocks above it. Such iron enrichment may represent iron that never settled into the core during the formation of the Earth or it may represent liquid iron that has diffused outward to form an alloy with the solid rocky mantle.

Is there a thin transition layer, perhaps like D″, on the *underside* of the mantle–core boundary? If there is, in the nomenclature of the last chapter, we could call this shell E'. Such a boundary layer at the top of a liquid in motion is common enough in everyday examples of convection; for the model of mantle convection, for example, the lithosphere can be thought of as a boundary layer at the top and D'' as a boundary layer at the bottom. We can at least ask, if there is a transition shell 50 to 100 km thick at the top of the liquid core, what effect would it have on seismic waves that might be detectable at observatories?

The most useful wave for explorations of elastic properties in the top of shell E is the wave *SKS*. This is the vertically polarized *S* wave that travels down through the mantle from the earthquake source, strikes the mantle–core boundary, and is refracted as a *P* wave (the *K* leg) into the liquid core. As shown in Figures 5.8(a) and (b), after traveling through the central core, it will eventually strike the underside of the mantle–core boundary and be refracted out into the mantle (partly as a *P* wave (not drawn in Figure 5.8) and partly as an *S* wave) back to the Earth's surface. If we follow only the *S* wave part of this ray, we have the complete wave *SKS*.

As an aid to understanding, a whole family of *SKS* rays has been plotted by the computer in Figure 5.8. The first *SKS* ray to penetrate the core occurs at a distance of between 60° and 70°. Before that, the *S* wave is totally internally reflected into the mantle as *ScS*. Beyond 70° the penetration into the core becomes greater and greater as the angle of incidence on the core boundary increases, so that *SKS* is detected at surface stations at distances out to 180°.

Let us do a numerical experiment on the computer to determine what happens if we change the properties slightly in E'. In Figure 5.8(a), the *P*-wave speed at the top of the core is taken to be 7.8 km/sec and increases smoothly to 8.5 km/sec at a depth of 100 km beneath the core boundary. In Figure 5.8(b), the velocity at the top of E' is taken to be 8.2 km/sec and again increases smoothly to 8.5 km/sec at a depth of 100 km in E'. Observe, however, the striking difference in the pattern of *SKS* rays. In Figure 5.8(a), the *SKS* rays in the core move out to greater distances more or less regularly from 70° to 80°, to 90°, and so on to 140°. By contrast, in Figure 5.8(b), the first refracted ray has swung out to 85° and the next member of the family has come *back* to 79°. Subsequently, the steeper and steeper SKS rays recede again to greater distances as in (a).

This recession and progression of the rays, with the formation of a caustic ring of strong illumination, has already been seen in the core—in the discussion of the last chapter of the *PKP* caustic (see Figure 4.7). In the case of E', we have a very striking example of the way that small variations in structure may have large consequences on the ray paths. Of course, this dramatic effect gives an opportunity to plan the earthquake probes so that *SKS* waves in the sensitive region between 70° and 90° can be studied. In principle, such observations should

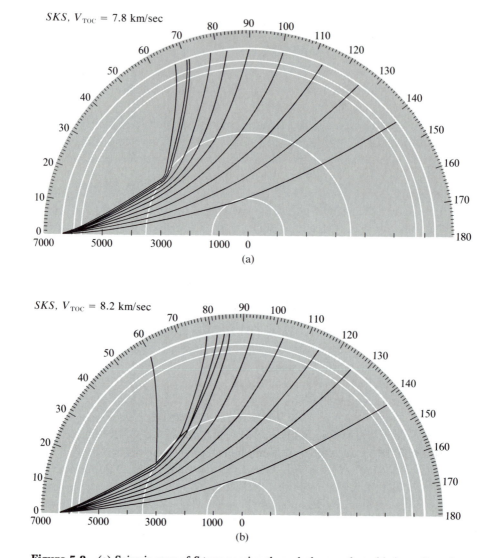

SKS, $V_{\text{TOC}} = 7.8$ km/sec

SKS, $V_{\text{TOC}} = 8.2$ km/sec

(a)

(b)

Figure 5.8 (a) Seismic rays of S type passing through the mantle and being reflected and refracted at the outer core boundary, producing the wave SKS at the surface. (Only the S legs in the mantle are shown.) The set of rays shown in this diagram are for a velocity at the top of the Earth's core of 7.8 km/sec. (b) A similar set of SKS rays. In this case, however, the velocity at the top of the Earth's core has been increased to 8.2 km/sec. The effect is to change the paths of the rays dramatically, causing the ray at approximately 85° to cross over rays to shorter distances, thus producing a cusp in the SKS travel-time curve and an increase in energy at this distance on the seismograms. [Courtesy of P. Murtha.]

allow us to discriminate between the two velocity models for E'. Unfortunately, there turns out to be, in this case, a major observational complication. The direct *S* wave through the mantle arrives at the stations between 70° and 80° a little before the *SKS* wave, and tends to mask the *SKS* onsets (see Box 3.2). A decision on the presence or absence of E' is thus difficult. Nevertheless, research along these lines is now progressing.

Inner Core Transition

Let us now focus our attention still deeper in the Earth. In particular consider the shell F (Figure 4.3). Even before 1940 the better-equipped seismological observatories reported tiny but clear *P*-wave precursors about 10 seconds before the main onset of the core waves *PKIKP* or *PKiKP* (see Figure 4.7) at distances between 130° and 140°. Attention was specially drawn to these curiosities, however, when quite unmistakable observations of precursor UEO's were reported on seismograms from the nuclear explosions at Bikini Atoll in 1954. A recent typical forerunner (see Figure 5.9) was generated by an earthquake near Java and recorded 132° away at a seismographic station in Golden, Colorado. The precursor waves arrived 17 seconds before the onset of the much stronger main *PKiKP* wave.

One straightforward explanation for these precursors occurred to me in 1962, and publication of the idea led to an involvement with exploration of the structure of the core that continues today. With personal involvement, as is well known, comes the danger of subjectivity, but the following account is an endeavor to be impartial (at any rate in the sense understood by the country judge who declared that he would lean neither to partiality on the one hand nor to impartiality on the other!).

My idea was that perhaps the wave velocities around the inner core were slightly but significantly different from the values that were contemplated at the time. Indeed, in 1962, there was complete disagreement between the velocity values for shell F given by Gutenberg and the estimates by Jeffreys. The former had a gradual but rapid change of *P* velocity spread over a hundred kilometers marking the boundary to the inner core, while the latter had a *decrease* in velocity followed by a sharp jump that defined the boundary. I suggested that between the inner and the outer core there was a transition shell, about 400 km wide, that had a very small jump in velocity (about 0.4 km/sec) at its upper boundary and then a constant velocity at deeper depths down to (like the Jeffreys solution) a *sharp* boundary to the inner core. (The reader should refer to the *P* velocity curve in

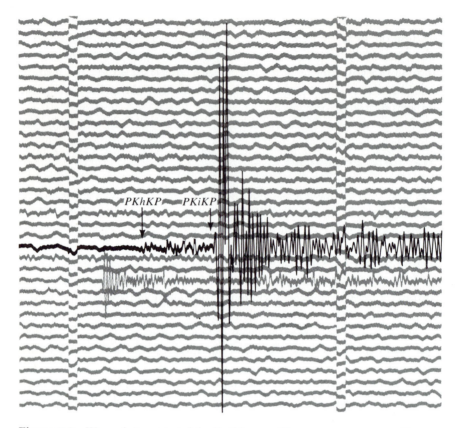

Figure 5.9   Waves that penetrated the Earth's core. These waves were created by a deep earthquake near Java and recorded at a distance of 132° by a seismograph at Golden, Colorado. The large-amplitude wave *PKiKP* was reflected from the Earth's solid inner core. It was preceded 17 seconds earlier by smaller *PKhKP* waves, which were probably scattered from the D'' shell or from the F shell. [From Bruce A. Bolt, "The Fine Structure of the Earth's Interior." Copyright © 1973 by Scientific American, Inc. All rights reserved.]

Figure 7.3.) After working out many mathematical models of the Earth's core I found that, although other explanations are possible, the hypothesis of such an F shell predicted travel times in reasonable agreement with all the available *PKP* observations, including the precursor waves. Independent studies by R. D. Adams and M. J. Randall at the Seismological Observatory in New Zealand, E. Engdahl at St. Louis, A. Qamar at Berkeley, and others tended to confirm the general results that I had obtained. The precursor waves reflected at or near the surface of the F shell were named *PKhKP*.

There were several fruits of my proposal of 1962. The demonstration that neither an anomalous *increase* (Gutenberg) nor *decrease* (Jeffreys) in velocity was required in F to fit the observation of *PKP* travel times removed problems concerning implausible changes in composition outside the inner core. Revised travel times for the core waves, based on my F shell model, not only helped other seismologists to find more examples of the small precursors but also helped in the search for the reflections (*PKiKP*) from the boundary of the inner core (see Chapter 4). These latter reflections led to the conclusions that the *inner* core has a sharp surface and that its radius is about 1216 km. By the end of the 1960's, it is fair to say, the old dichotomy between the Gutenberg and Jeffreys solutions had been swept away to be replaced by a model of a transition F shell of width about 400 km and only small, if any, changes in elastic properties throughout.

The quiet did not last. An alternative explanation of radically different kind for the precursor waves was hit on by R. A. W. Haddon in Australia in 1972. He suggested that they are *PKP* waves scattered at or near the *mantle–core boundary* and that they are *not* caused by structure in an F transition zone at all. The scattering would take place principally from points where the caustic surface of *PKP* (discussed in Chapter 4), at which the wave energy is high, intersects the outer boundary of the liquid core (in other words, from the places on the mantle–core boundary where the *PKP* rays that reach the surface near 142° are refracted (see Figure 4.3)).

The stimulus to reexamine the hypothesis of reflections from a sharp surface at the top of shell F that I had suggested in 1962 led to seismologists searching for observations, not only of travel times, but also of amplitudes of the faint *PKhKP* waves. Such amplitudes, as seen in Figure 5.9, are very tiny—much smaller than predicted from a velocity jump as large as 0.4 km/sec between shell E and shell F. This problem troubled a number of observers, and it was demonstrated in 1972 by A. Qamar at the annual meeting of the Seismological Society of America that the observed and predicted amplitudes could be reconciled if the jump in seismic *P* velocity in F were reduced by a factor of twenty (to about 0.01 km/sec). On this interpretation, simple ray theory would still hold, but *PKhKP* forerunners would now be associated with reflections or upward scattering from relatively minor structural complexities at the top of F.

At the University of Sydney, Haddon by 1970 had also begun to seek an explanation of the *PKP* precursors that would satisfy the amplitude as well as all the other data, and decided that the F shell hypothesis had some holes in it. Among other difficulties was the problem of accounting for the arrival of UEO's between the *PKhKP* onset and that of *PKiKP*, as is seen for example in Figure 5.9. What would account for this background energy?

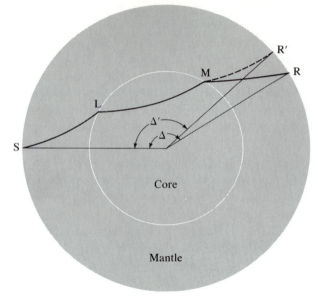

(a)

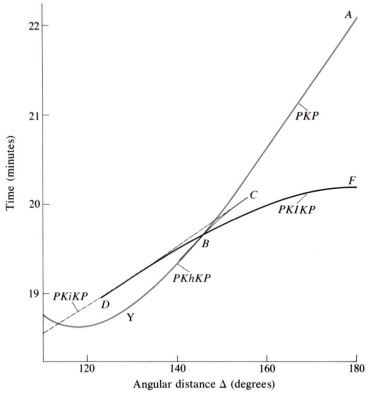

(b)

For the rest of the story, it is best perhaps to follow, with some simplifications, a clear account of the new hypothesis that emerged at Sydney, given in 1973 by K. E. Bullen and Haddon himself. By apparent exhaustion of plausible possibilities, in due course the idea arose that the *PKP* precursor readings are not associated primarily with any internal discontinuities inside the outer or inner core such as shell F, but with *scattering* of waves near the mantle–core boundary. To illustrate the thesis simply, let us artificially restrict consideration to rays and other paths lying inside a single diametral plane of the Earth as in Figure 5.10(a). Scattering outside this plane may be significant but does not affect the essential results to be described.

Let S be the source of an earthquake and let SLMR be the pencil of *PKP* rays whose lowest points are inside the outer core, the legs SL and MR being in the mantle and the segment LM in the core. The rays emerge at angular distances Δ, where Δ is greater than the distance of the caustic near 142°. Being rays, these paths satisfy Snell's law (corresponding to least time) throughout their lengths.

Now consider a path SLMR' emerging at distances Δ', with the following properties: the portion SLM is identical with that for the ray SLMR; the upward mantle segment MR' (and hence the recording point) varies continuously producing many rays; Snell's law applies throughout each path except at the point M of upward refraction. Figure 5.10(a) shows a particular ray of the family SLMR, and a member SLMR' of the corresponding subsidiary family of paths for which there is scattering at M.

The full family of paths SLMR covers the possibilities due to scattering taking place at the mantle–core boundary. For each given SLM ray we can easily draw a single scattering curve, called Y say, of travel time T against distance Δ. The full travel-time curve for the *PKP* waves (without a region F) is drawn in Figure 5.10(b). The curve Y extends back from the point corresponding to variations in MR paths into the shadow zone at distances less than 142°. Because MR' is shorter than MR, the travel time for the scattered ray SLMR' will be less than for the regular refracted ray SLMR. Figure 5.10(b) shows the curve Y, which gives for all distances Δ the minimum arrival times due to the assumed form of scattering at the boundary between the mantle and the core.

Figure 5.10   (a) SLMR, a typical member of the family of ordinary *PKP* rays whose lowest points are in the outer core. SLMR' is a member of an associated family of paths for which there is scattering at M. (b) *PKP* phases and scattering curve Y for scattering at points M at angular distance of 117.5° from the focus. The curve Y gives the theoretical minimum arrival times due to the assumed form of scattering.

Observations of travel times of the precursor *PKhKP* waves such as those in Figure 5.9 generally do fall in between the curve *Y* and the curve called DF (*PKIKP* waves) in Figure 5.10(b), and the minimum-time curve *Y* which corresponds to the ray SLMR at 142° (point B), agrees reasonably well with the earliest arrival times of the precursors.

Bullen and Haddon conclude that "The agreement between theory and observation is further supported from a comparison of expected amplitude variations and observations of particular precursor wave trains. Since the theoretical curve *Y* involves scattering only at a single point M, the arrivals corresponding to this particular curve, i.e., the earliest arrivals, are expected to have smaller amplitudes than later arrivals since the latter involve the superposition of waves scattered from a series of points M." The reader can confirm to what extent the seismogram in Figure 5.9 has UEO's between *PKhKP* and *PKiKP* that conform to this property. (It is sometimes not the case.)

This short description must conclude the present account of the two hypotheses explaining the precursors to the core waves. Perhaps most people could hardly conceive scientists devoting so much time and attention to such remote and esoteric problems. In fact, the interpretations do have implications for physicists working on the state of material at the great pressures of the interior, on the generation of Earth's magnetism, and on the geodynamical forces of geological processes.

Before leaving the subject, however, it only remains to comment that in the years since 1972, different types of observations from those discussed here using the giant seismic arrays discussed in Chapter 3 have established that many of the *PKhKP* precursors apparently do travel with speeds required for paths like the scattered ray SLMR'. (Some evidence from array studies also indicates that some precursors are associated with shell F.) On the other hand, there is considerable controversy as to the nature of the scattering: some seismologists hold that the scattering at M is due to a rash of "bumps" on the core boundary; others hold that it is rather "lumps" in the transition shell D" that do the trick. The safest present position seems to be that the faint forerunners to the earthquake waves that pass through the Earth's core are the sum of waves reflected or scattered from rough structure *both* near to the mantle–core boundary and outside the inner core boundary.

Hugo Benioff (1899–1968)
"The physical science of seismology is based almost entirely on [earthquake] observations made with seismographs and clocks."

CHAPTER 6

Earth Vibrations

Observations from Great Earthquakes

Sometimes earthquakes cause the Earth to ring like a bell. High-magnitude earthquakes contain sufficient energy to vibrate the whole planet and produce the deep-toned music of our terrestrial sphere. Imagine the excitement among seismologists when, after the massive Chilean earthquakes of May 1960, for the first time the few very long-period seismographs around the world were seen clearly to record extremely long-period waves for many days!

One of these instruments, constructed by A. Marussi for tidal measurements, consisted of two great pendulums suspended from the ceiling of an underground limestone cavern, the Grotta Gigante, in Trieste, Italy. They had a free period of 2 minutes and recorded horizontal motions of the ground. The record from one of these pendulums is reproduced in Figure 6.1, and earthquake vibrations of predominantly 8 minute period are clearly visible for over 16 hours. These vibrations are superimposed on much longer periodicities; these very long waves are the tides of the solid Earth with periods of about 12 and 24 hours.

Tidal motions, due to the mutual attraction of the Earth, Moon, and Sun, are of course always with us. The tides of the elastic Earth played a role in early arguments by Lord Kelvin and Sir George Darwin on the rigidity of the terrestrial interior (Chapter 1). The amplitudes of the solid Earth tides are quite large (but imperceptible to the human senses because of their long wavelength and slowness), amounting to 20 cm or so each day. Although study of these tides, which

May 23, 1960

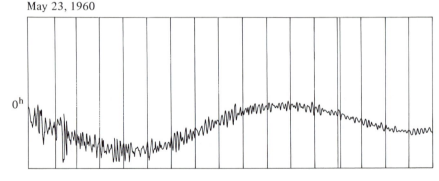

0^h

Figure 6.1   Portion of the Trieste N-S horizontal pendulum record from the tiltmeter in the Grotta Gigante following the great Chilean earthquake of May 22, 1960. Vertical lines mark hourly intervals.

can be looked on as continued *forced* vibrations of the globe, is an important branch of geophysics and gives valuable clues on the broad nature of the interior, we will not give an account of them in this book. We cannot stray so far from the earthquake highway.

Analysis of 1960 Chile earthquake records like that in Figure 6.1 gave the first unequivocal evidence that free vibrations of the Earth had, in fact, been generated. Mathematicians had from the eighteenth century worked on vibrations of an elastic sphere, and in 1911 A. E. H. Love, commemorated by the Love surface wave, predicted that a steel sphere as large as the Earth would have a period of fundamental (gravest) vibration of about 1 hour, and there would be overtones with lesser periods. The matter rested as a theoretical curiosity until 1954 when Professor Hugo Benioff, already mentioned in Chapter 5, announced that he had detected an oscillation of period 57 minutes in a seismogram of the great Kamchatka earthquake of November 4, 1952.

The robust observational proof demanded by the skeptics came, however, from instrumental recording in North and South America, Europe, and Japan following the 1960 Chilean earthquake. I well remember my own enormous delight in carrying through the mathematical search for the Earth's free tones in the Trieste record shown in Figure 6.1. The work was done at Cambridge University, England, in early 1961, and my curiosity was rewarded as I plotted the computer output that showed the telltale peaks in the spectrum. The periods of the largest peaks fell very close to theoretical values calculated previously for a plausible model of the Earth. Seismologists at other places, working with other records, had the same experience, and we all realized that a completely new part of seismology had been born. It was to be named *terrestrial spectroscopy*.

The longest or gravest period of vibration measured was 54.0 minutes with many peaks corresponding to faster types of vibration. Observed Earth spectra, like that in Figure 6.2(b) clearly indicate that, like the rich tones of a tolling bell, the resonant vibrations of the Earth have many harmonics, all adding together to produce at a particular observatory on the surface a complex motion. The challenge is to disentangle the separate modes and then measure their individual amplitudes, frequencies, and phases. We then have a chance to identify them against some internationally accepted nomenclature and compare results with those of others. We will develop this name system in the next section.

The final step is, as always in probing the Earth, to tackle the inverse problem explained in the first chapter. In the case of the Earth's resonant vibrations, this problem can be simply stated. If we knew the physical properties inside the Earth, as we might know the density and elasticity of a brass bell, we could calculate in the same way as Love from the appropriate mathematics the expected frequencies and amplitude pattern for the resonant vibrations. (Although, because there is really an infinite number of such modes, even to this statement we should add "in principle.") This calculation is the direct or forward problem. Indeed, this forward calculation has been done for many surmised models of the Earth's interior and, nowadays, if a speculative model of the planet is to be taken seriously, its resonant spectra must not violate observed spectra such as that in Figure 6.2. This comparison is crucial in detective work on the Earth but is often regarded as "second best." In a deeper way, unquestionably we face a problem in which procedures must be the reverse of those above. Starting with the observed vibrations we must try to *construct* a structure and elastic properties for the inaccessible interior that will produce tones with frequencies in agreement with the observed ones.

In fact, we can never do this exactly. Theorems have been proved that show that, because we cannot measure each and every one of the infinite number of harmonics produced when an earthquake strikes, we can never resolve exactly and uniquely the physical nature of the vibrating Earth. Fortunately, other theorems hold out the hope that, with some additional assumptions and data, we can get close to the true picture (and we always have the "second best" method of trial and error). These questions of uniqueness and resolution will be recognized at once by all who struggle with observational work. They constitute some of the most intriguing and as yet intractable challenges in modern science.

After 1960, many more spectra of Earth's resonant oscillations were obtained from a variety of great earthquakes. Of particular importance was the destructive Good Friday earthquake in 1964, magnitude 8.6, that had its epicenter in Prince William Sound, Alaska. In this case over 100 seismographic stations around the world with long-period seismographs recorded the whole Earth vibrations, thus

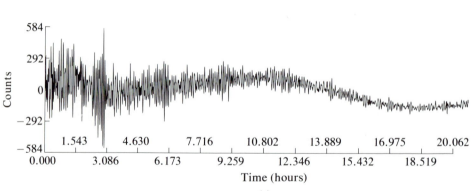

(a)

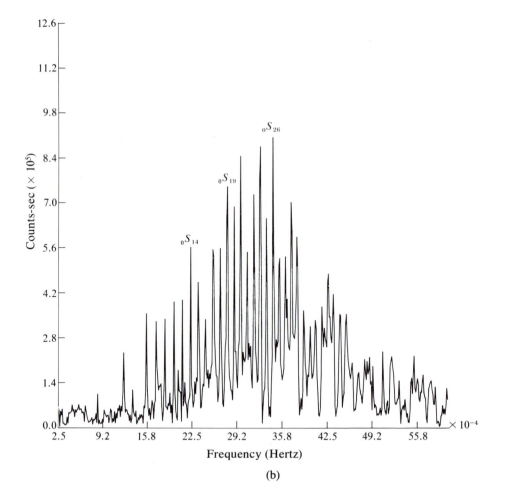

(b)

confirming their global nature. A recent study used records from a broad-band pendulum seismograph at Whiskeytown, California. The seismogram (time domain) of the vertical ground motion following the Indonesia earthquake of August 19, 1977, is shown in Figure 6.2(a), and the corresponding elegant spectrum (frequency domain) is reproduced in Figure 6.2(b).

Terrestrial Spectroscopy

We need a convenient way to describe simply the resonant vibrations of the terrestrial globe. First, we should emphasize that we are dealing with vibrations that continue in an unforced way (after the earthquake source releases its energy) with frequencies that depend only upon properties of the elastic globe itself. The exact analogy is a plucked stringed instrument (see Box 6.1) from which, as the Greeks recognized more than a thousand years ago, come musical harmonics that depend only on the length, density, and tautness of the plucked string. Such free oscillations, mentioned in Chapter 3, are called *eigenvibrations*.

Second, there are two and only two separate types of eigenvibrations of an elastic sphere. This property was first proved in 1882 by the English mathematician Sir Horace Lamb in one of his fundamental theoretical contributions to seismology. In one type, now called *S* modes or *spheroidal vibrations,* the displacements of elements of the sphere have, in general, components along the radius as well as horizontal. In fact, the particle orbits are just like those in Rayleigh waves (Figure 2.4); in other words, we find here a dual relation between the standing spheroidal vibrations and the traveling Rayleigh waves.

Also, there are *T* or *torsional vibrations* (sometimes called "toroidal" vibrations but this name is unsuitable since the displacements do not resemble doughnuts). These have tangential but no radial displacements and are dual to Love waves. Similarly to *P* and *S* waves, spheroidal and torsional oscillations generally occur together so that the motion of any point on the surface is a mix of both types.

Since last century, astronomers have also been familiar with eigenvibrations of spheres in their considerations of massive pulsating and rotating stars. They

---

Figure 6.2   (a) Recording of Earth vibrations and tidal oscillations after the great Indonesia earthquake of August 19, 1977 (magnitude 7.9). This vertical ground motion was measured at Whiskeytown Station of the University of California, Berkeley. (b) Frequency spectrum calculated from the seismogram in (a). Each sharp peak corresponds to a separate mode of oscillation. Three spheroidal *S* modes are identified. [Courtesy of R. A. Hansen.]

are interested not only in measuring the frequencies of the light pulse from these distant celestial objects, but also in whether such stars remain stable under vibrational forces. Physicists are also at home with terrestrial spectroscopy because of its close similarity to the vibrational mechanics of atoms. At least in this field, quantum mechanics and seismology come close together and, as we will see in the next section, the atomic analogy has proved valuable in dealing with the fine spectra of a spinning Earth.

The nomenclature for the T and S modes is easy to grasp. It depends upon describing the pattern of motions in terms of the meshwork of nodal surfaces—or places where no motion takes place. As Box 6.1 illustrates, there is in general a series of nodal lines on the surface of the Earth (see second diagram), more or less corresponding to lines of latitude and longitude on a globe. If a seismograph on the surface is on a nodal line of a particular mode, then it will not record that mode. There will be also, in general, spherical surfaces *inside* the Earth where the various modes of vibration have no displacement (see third diagram). Clearly the description of each mode, just as for the vibrating string, will depend on a count of the nodal surfaces and we will use the letters n and l to indicate the counts at depth and on the surface, respectively.

Because they are the least complicated consider first the torsional vibrations. In terms of numbers n and l related to the numbers of nodal lines, we write $_nT_l$. The suffix n denotes the number of internal nodal surfaces (the one at the Earth's center is not counted), and l is one more than the number of surface nodal lines, i.e., it equals the number of separate sectors on the surface.

The simplest torsional oscillation $_0T_2$ is drawn in Figure 6.3. There is only one nodal surface that cuts the surface in the equator and the north and south hemispheres twist in opposite directions. Motion in the same sense extends throughout the interior.* This mode is the *fundamental* torsional eigenvibration of the Earth. On the top right of Figure 6.3 is sketched the first *radial* overtones of the fundamental T mode. In this case, called $_1T_2$, there is still only one *surface* nodal line ($l = 2$) but there is also one interior (or radial) surface (n) across which the motion changes direction. The sketch shows that there are now four separate parts to the pulsating motion, each moving in different directions relative to its neighbor. It is fascinating to imagine a rubber ball vibrating in this way!

Now, let us describe the corresponding notation $_nS_l$ for S modes. In this case, for which vertical displacements occur, the fundamental vibration $_0S_2$ resembles the alternate up-and-down and sideways bulging of an elastic football. This alter-

---

*For the moment, ignore the presence of a liquid core in the Earth, and assume it is a simple nonrotating elastic sphere.

Box 6.1   Vibrations of Strings and Spheres

The figure below shows the modes of vibration of a string. The string moves from the position shown in black to the position shown in gray, and back again. The nodes are the points that do not move.

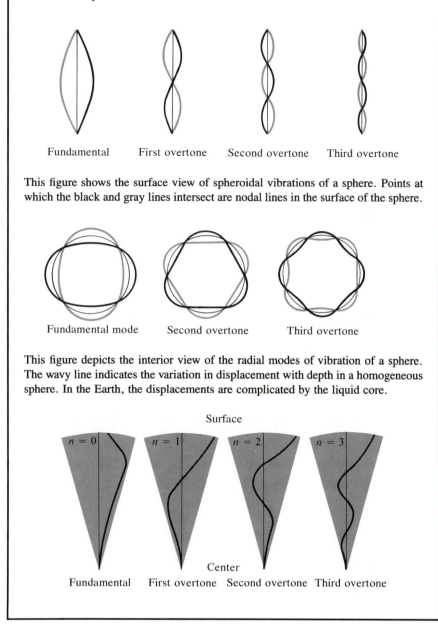

Fundamental	First overtone	Second overtone	Third overtone

This figure shows the surface view of spheroidal vibrations of a sphere. Points at which the black and gray lines intersect are nodal lines in the surface of the sphere.

Fundamental mode	Second overtone	Third overtone

This figure depicts the interior view of the radial modes of vibration of a sphere. The wavy line indicates the variation in displacement with depth in a homogeneous sphere. In the Earth, the displacements are complicated by the liquid core.

Surface

$n = 0$ $n = 1$ $n = 2$ $n = 3$

Center

Fundamental	First overtone	Second overtone	Third overtone

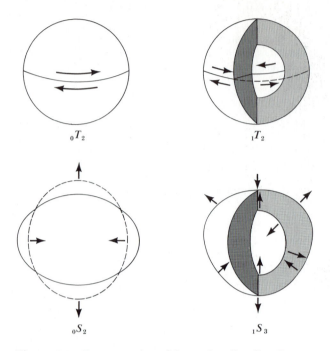

Figure 6.3   Representation of the modes $_0T_2$, $_1T_2$, $_0S_2$, and $_1S_3$.

native bulging is shown in the lower left corner of Figure 6.3 and in the second diagram of Box 6.1. Thus, here are *two* surface nodal lines which correspond to latitude lines in the north and south hemispheres for $_0S_2$, in accord with the rule for spheroidal oscillations that the suffix l equals the number of surface nodal lines. The two surface overtones $_0S_3$ and $_0S_4$ are also drawn in the middle diagram of Box 6.1. It is readily checked that they have 3 and 4 nodal latitude lines, respectively.

Of course, as with torsional modes, there can also be *internal* nodal surfaces and the subscript n is again a measure of the number of these. In the bottom right corner of Figure 6.1, the first radial overtone $_1S_3$ is illustrated.

In summary, we describe the T modes and S modes for a spherical, elastic, solid, nonrotating Earth by the symbols $_nT_l$ and $_nS_l$. The first integer, n, specifies the pattern of vibrations with depth, and the second, l, fixes the surface or angular pattern of displacements. Because both n and l can take values from zero to infinity, there is a double infinity of possible modes, but observationally we are concerned only with values of n and l less than a few hundred.

From the drawings in Box 6.1 it is obvious that as the values of n and l increase, the numbers of radial and angular nodal surfaces become more closely spaced. At the same time the frequency of the oscillations increases. With a little imagination, we can visualize trains of surface waves traveling backward and forward over the Earth's surface (see Figure 3.5). and producing the pattern of standing waves that we call eigenvibrations. The traveling Rayleigh waves would finally superimpose to produce the S modes, and the traveling Love waves would add to produce the T modes.

A specially simple case of S modes occurs when there is no nodal surface anywhere in the Earth. This vibration, called $_0S_0$, occurs when all parts of the Earth just pulse in and out like the balloon on an oxygen mask. It is the exact analog of the radial pulsations of a distant star.

Many measurements of the frequencies of T and S modes are now available, even though the first definite observations occurred only in 1960. A few values of these spectral values for the gravest modes are of interest (see Box 6.2). Because the wavelengths of the longest vibrations are so great, even longer than the radius of the Earth, the frequencies involved are very small, and it is less awkward to give the values in terms of period of vibration (see Box 1.2). The eigenperiods of $_0S_2$, $_0S_3$, and $_0S_4$ are found to be approximately 54, 35, and 25 minutes, respectively. The actual longest eigenperiod of the Earth that is observed (54 minutes for $_0S_2$) is thus about 6 minutes shorter than that predicted theoretically 70 years ago by Love for a uniform Earth. The difference is, of course, a measure of the deviation of the real Earth from uniform conditions.

The period of the pure radial oscillation $_0S_0$ is 20.5 minutes. The spectrum of torsional modes $_nT_l$ has periods with values that overlap the measured values for the S family. For example, the periods for $_0T_{20}$ and $_0S_{19}$ are 360.3 and 360.2 seconds, respectively. The free periods are, in fact, measured to more decimal places than given here, but to make use of the greater observational precision that is now available we must shift from a gross to a finer description of the spectra.

Effect of Earth's Asymmetries

The story of the terrestrial eigenvibrations is even more eventful than indicated in the last section. We are here at the boundary of present-day research, and curiosity demands that we pursue this rich vein just a little further. The present challenge is evident in Figure 6.4. This spectral plot shows vividly that there is a fine structure present in the longest resonant vibration of the Earth $_0S_2$ (or the

Box 6.2   Damping in the Earth

If a damped oscillating sphere has a frequency f (hertz), then the amplitude A of the oscillation decays exponentially from an original amplitude A_o with time t:

$$A = A_o \exp(-\beta t) \tag{1}$$

where

$$\beta = \pi f/Q \tag{2}$$

From (1) and (2):
  (a) the higher the frequency, the greater the damping,
  (b) the higher the attenuation factor Q, the less the damping.

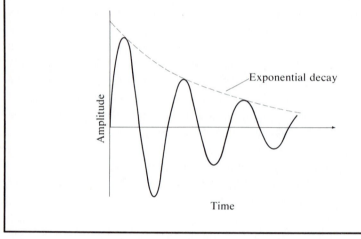

"football" mode) after the 1960 Chilean earthquake. Rather than a single peak, as seen for each mode in Figure 6.2, it proved possible in this case to resolve the harmonics near a period of 53.8 minutes into fine details. Five close neighbors are marked with arrows in Figure 6.4 and there can be no argument about the reality of at least three of them. The difference in frequencies between the longest and shortest vibrations in this multiplet is a few percent, which is quite significant. We must seek an explanation.

Now it turns out that theory predicts that any deviation from the perfect conditions of elasticity and sphericity assumed in the last section will always *split*

Eigenperiod and Q estimates for some T and S modes.

Mode	Period (sec)	Q
$_0T_2$	2638	350
$_0T_4$	1303	300
$_0T_5$	1076	250
$_0T_{10}$	619	190
$_0T_{15}$	452	170
$_0S_2$	3233	620
$_0S_6$	963	480
$_0S_{12}$	502	370
$_0S_{19}$	360	270
$_0S_{24}$	306	240
$_0S_0$	1228	5000
$_1T_2$	757	
$_2T_4$	420	
$_1S_3$	1064	
$_4S_5$	415	
$_5S_0$	205	

the spectral lines. Rather than a single vibration $_nT_l$ or $_nS_l$, each is opened into a multiplet of vibrations nestled around the original vibration. It is like seeing a closed hand open into 4 fingers and a thumb. Let us list the deviations that are the main culprits. First, the Earth is not a perfect sphere, but is elliptical. What effect does this have on the terrestrial spectra? The answer is not very much but enough to be observed for the longest oscillations using the very best analysis of seismograms after great earthquakes. The extreme shift in this case in the frequencies of the split multiplet is of order 1 percent and is most severe with the gravest modes.

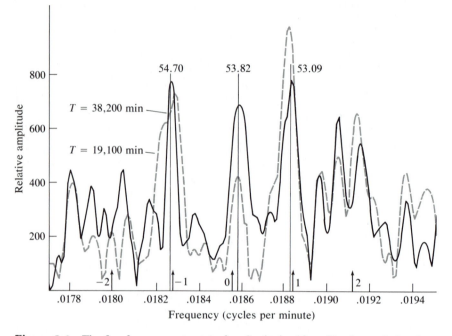

Figure 6.4   The fine frequency structure for $_0S_2$ obtained by a Fourier analysis of two lengths of record, 19,100 and 38,200 minutes from the Isabella strain meter after the Chilean earthquake of May 22, 1960. Sample interval is 2 minutes. Theoretical splitting from the rotation of the Earth is marked on the base line. [Courtesy of S. W. Smith, 1961.]

Another asymmetry of the Earth is the position of continents and oceans. Seventy percent of the Earth's surface is covered by oceans and most are in the southern hemisphere. One of the major questions about the Earth that has not yet been fully answered is: how do the relative positions of the continents, tectonic zones, and oceans affect the eigenvibrations? A partial answer from model studies of a vibrating complex Earth, using a computer, shows that these tectonic complexities do split each peak in the resonant T and S spectra. Further, the ground displacements at any place in each separate vibration of the multiplet are oriented in a way that depends upon the distribution of the great tectonic structures such as continents.

The way that the continent–ocean contrast changes the directions of the surface displacements is illustrated dramatically in Figure 6.5. This computer generated picture shows the surface ground motions as small arrows for the mode $_0T_5$. For a homogeneous Earth, all the small vectors would be parallel to latitude lines.

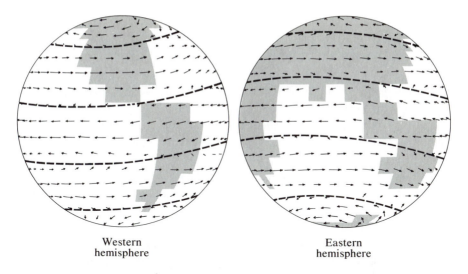

Western
hemisphere

Eastern
hemisphere

Figure 6.5   The western and eastern hemispheres of a vibrating
Earth. The outlines of the continents are shown with gray shadings.
The small arrows represent the direction and amplitude of
displacements on the surface of the Earth in the free oscillation $_0T_5$.
This oscillation has five zones of motion on the surface, separated by
four meridians shown as dashed lines. On these nodal lines there is no
surface displacement. If the Earth were a homogeneous surface with no
structural contrast between ocean and continents, the small vectors
would lie parallel to the nodal lines. In fact, however, their tails vary in
direction because of the structural complexities of the Earth. [Courtesy
of J. Stifler.]

This is clearly not the case for the model used that includes continents. For the
torsional oscillations $_0T_2$ to $_0T_{10}$, however, the effects of the Earth's ellipticity
are greater than the effects of the structural contrasts between continents and
oceans. The splitting induced by the latter effect is probably no more than a few
tenths of a percent for the graver modes but, as we climb the ladder of overtones,
the importance of continent–ocean contrasts increases.

A related result of importance to earthquake observatories endeavoring to
detect the T and S modes is that, if the hyperfine spectral structure such as shown
in Figure 6.4 is not resolved, the apparent eigenfrequency of a mode will depend
on the geographical relation of the station. For example, for the mode $_0T_{10}$
recorded at the South Pole, the relative amplitudes of the individual members of
the multiplet caused by ellipticity and tectonic contrasts emphasize the higher
frequencies. Biased estimates of the eigenfrequencies could thus easily result.

So far we have not found an effect large enough to explain the splitting of 5 percent in $_0S_2$ shown in Figure 6.4. The asymmetry that does explain most of it is more subtle than the two cases already described. It is the asymmetry that arises from the forces acting on the Earth due to the Earth's rotation. It is as though we were listening to a drum being played on a stage that revolved at a high speed. The main splitting effect is thus dynamical and not geometrical. Students of physics will see in this phenomenon a mechanical analogy to the famous splitting of atomic spectral lines by a magnetic field, discovered by Zeeman in 1896. The rotational splitting dominates the fine spectrum of the gravest modes since these effectively have elastic motions through the whole bulk of the Earth. For $_0S_2$ (Figure 6.4) and $_0T_2$, the variation in period reaches several percent from this cause.

In summary, there is a trade-off between the effects of the various asymmetries on the Earth's resonant vibrations. The very-long-period modes (e.g., $_0T_2$, $_0S_2$) that vibrate the bulk of the Earth are most affected by rotation; as the order of the overtone increases (e.g., $_0T_{20}$, $_0S_{20}$), the motion is confined more and more to the upper part of the Earth, and the ellipticity and tectonic contrasts begin to dominate. In the next decade, with better equipment and more great earthquakes, it should prove possible to be more definitive about the terrestrial hyperfine spectra.

Measurements of Damping

We have still ignored one key property of Earth vibrations that is quite obvious in Figure 6.1. There it can be seen that the free vibrations gradually die away as they ride upon the forced tidal motions. On the Trieste record in 1960, it took two days before the ultralong waves became invisible. In more recent great earthquakes, specially designed seismographs have detected certain modes for weeks before they are lost in the background microseisms. Instruments of the International Deployment of Accelerometers (IDA, see Chapter 3) now hold the record for the longest recording of an S mode—about 3 weeks for $_0S_0$.

Nevertheless, ultimately the resonant vibrations always are lost to observation as their energy is sapped by frictional forces. In other words, the mechanical vibrational energy is slowly dissipated into heat energy by nonelastic processes in the interior. Naturally, we are interested in measuring these nonelastic processes because of the light they throw on the evolution of the structure and dynamics of the Earth.

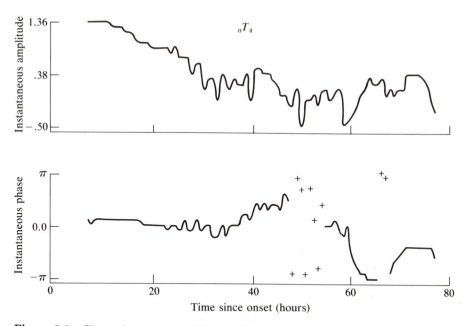

Figure 6.6   Change in amplitude of the oscillation $_0T_4$ with time after the Earth has commenced to vibrate. After about 30 hours the amplitude becomes quite irregular, indicating that the signal has diminished to about the level of the background noise. In the lower diagram the phase of the oscillation is plotted against the time after the earthquake onset. The phase remains more or less constant till about 30 hours when it again becomes irregular in agreement with the amplitude diagram. We conclude that the oscillation is not being clearly detected after this time.

Most decaying systems in nature follow an exponential curve (see Box 6.2), and the amplitudes of decaying oscillations of the Earth appear to be no exception. In addition, the general observed rule is that the greater the frequency of oscillation the higher is the decay rate. In Box 6.2, the well-known mathematical form for this type of attenuation is written explicitly in terms of the frequency of the mode of vibration and a damping factor called Q. The simple assumption is that a Q factor can be assigned to each mode in such a way that large values of Q entail small rates of decay, while small Q values mean high attentuation. The question is: how is Q best measured for each S and T mode?

The recommended approach is illustrated by Figure 6.6 and involves passing freely back and forth from free Earth vibrations in time into the world of the frequency domain as described in Chapter 1. The first step is to isolate the mode of interest by selecting a peak and its corresponding frequency in the eigenspectrum. Suppose we choose $_0S_{19}$ in Figure 6.2(b). Then we go back to the original recorded data, like that in Figure 6.2(a), and at each instant of time we calculate the amplitude and phase of the pure $_0S_{19}$ vibration as one component of all the mix of vibrations actually present. Of course, even with a high-speed computer, this process of moving from start to finish of the record is rather time-consuming; the advantage is that we are working from first principles.

Typical results of the computation of amplitude and phase are plotted in Figure 6.6 in the case of the $_0T_4$ mode as recorded by the Trieste N–S horizontal pendulum after the 1960 Chilean earthquake. The upper curve gives the relative amplitude of the ground displacement as time went on for over 70 hours. The decay in amplitude is clearly evident during the first 30 hours, but thereafter the amplitude of ground motion fluctuates rather wildly. The bottom curve shows that this $_0T_4$ vibration remains *in phase* also for about 30 hours, but thereafter the phase begins to change rapidly. We can conclude that the Trieste instrument only picked up the $_0T_4$ vibration for 30 hours at levels not obscured by microseismic and other noise, and consequently any measurements of $_0T_4$ made from this record should be confined to this time interval.

After this crucial decision, we can return to the top curve of Figure 6.6 and measure the rate of decay of amplitude during the first 30 hours. (With the scale used, the slope of the instantaneous amplitude line is proportional to the β in equation (1) of Box 6.2.) When this is done, the corresponding Q value is about 300 (see the table in Box 6.2). We can then repeat this process for other modes of the spectra.

In practice, it has proved difficult to measure the Q values very precisely for a number of reasons that need not keep us here. (One obvious reason is that the aftershocks of great earthquakes continue to add energy to the resonant shaking of the Earth.) In general, however, the Q values for each mode are different with magnitudes ranging from 5000 for the persistent $_0S_0$ mode to a few hundreds for the longer period $_0T_l$ and $_0S_l$ modes. Usually, T modes have lower Q values (i.e., more damping) than S modes possessing about the same frequency, and as the order l of the surface overtones increases (i.e., the eigenperiod decreases), the Q values fall.

The reason for the change of the damping factors Q as the order of each overtone changes is, of course, evident when we take into account the different distribution of displacement of the material throughout the Earth in each mode (see Box 6.1). Graver modes, for instance, have motions that penetrate more deeply into the body of the Earth than higher modes. Hence, the values of Q for the graver modes tell us more about the damping properties of the deeper parts

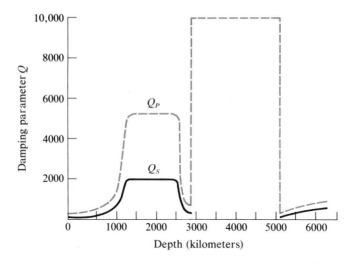

Figure 6.7 Average estimates for the damping parameters Q_P
and Q_S in the Earth's interior. In the lower mantle, Q_P and Q_S
rise to reasonably high values. In the liquid core there is only a
P wave, and this suffers very little damping, with a Q of order
10,000.

of the Earth. Indeed, we can systematically work our way down the ladder of
modes and allocate average Q values to the layers inside the Earth from the upper
mantle to the inner core.

The differences in Q values between T and S modes are not only related to the
different distribution of motions with depth but also the physical nature of the
two types of vibrations. As we have already noted, the torsional modes arise from
shearing motions, as in Love and S waves, while the rocks are both compressed
and sheared in spheroidal modes, similarly to Rayleigh and P waves. For this
reason, two separate damping factors are required, called Q_P and Q_S, which
correspond to damping of P-type motions and damping of S-type motions,
respectively.

Once again, it will be clear that the detective work needed to find damping
factors with depth in the Earth is an example of turning the usual direct problem
inside out. If we knew Q_P and Q_S in the Earth, we could *calculate* directly the
damping of earthquake waves and resonant vibrations. On the contrary, we have
the observed damping and require the attentuation factors. The solution, unfortunately, is not straightforward and, indeed, many solutions may be hazarded.

In Figure 6.7 we see one recent suggestion for the values of Q_P and Q_S inside
the globe. This solution has the damping for S waves greater than that for P waves

at every corresponding depth. In the middle mantle, both Q factors rise significantly (i.e., low energy dissipation there), while at the bottom of the mantle in the shell D'', both factors fall. Because the outer core is liquid, no S waves propagate and Q_S equals zero. In sharp contrast, as we saw with *PKKKKKKKP* waves in Chapter 5, P waves suffer little attenuation and Q_P may be as high as 10,000 in the liquid core. This solution follows work of D. L. Anderson and R. S. Hart at the Seismological Laboratory at Cal Tech in 1978.

In the inner core, Q_P falls again to values similar to those in the upper mantle and, as yet, Q_S near the center is a question mark. The average Q_P value in the inner core is given in Figure 6.7 as near 450. As it turns out, we have a close check from the unique observation of *PKIIKP* waves (Figures 4.8 and 4.9) discussed in Chapter 4. As Figure 4.9 shows, the *PKIIKP* wave with two legs in the inner core has a longer period (i.e., higher frequencies missing) than the corresponding *PKiKP* wave. As I demonstrated in 1980 this observed difference requires Q_P in the inner core to be in the range 350 to 550. The check with the Figure 6.7 estimate is close, at least for high-frequency P waves.

Francis Birch (b. 1903)
*"The only information about definite levels of the
[Earth's] interior, derived from seismology, has an
abstract character and requires deciphering."*

CHAPTER 7

Densities, Elastic Properties, and Temperatures

Density from Seismic Velocities

What is Earth made of? One way to determine an unknown material is by means of its density. The units of density common a few years ago were grams per cubic centimeter (g/cm^3). Nowadays the standard unit is kilograms per cubic meter (see Table 1 in the Appendix), but we will simplify matters by dropping the units and referring all densities to the density of water taken to be 1 g/cm^3. At normal temperatures and pressures, aluminum is a light solid metal (density 2.7) whereas mercury is a dense liquid one (density 13.6). Marble is a relatively light rock (density 2.7) whereas eclogite (density 3.4) is a relatively heavy one. A key, then, to the composition of the deep interior would be a knowledge of the density.

In the pre-seismological age, geophysicists struggled to get an idea of the distribution of density from the surface to the center using the small amount of data available to them, such as the densities of representative surface rocks (Chapter 1). Two key physical measurements not dependent on seismology were the average *density* (5.52) of the whole Earth (obtained by dividing the total mass by the volume of the Earth) and its *moment of inertia*. The latter is important because the distribution of density throughout the terrestrial sphere fixes the inertia of the sphere about its axis (see Box 7.1). From these few data, a plausible conclusion is that the Earth's density increases from about 2.5 at the surface to between 10 and 15 at the center.

Box 7.1   Mass and Moment of Inertia of the Earth

Mass of the Earth $M = 5.973 \times 10^{24}$ kg

Corresponding mean density $D = 5.515$ g/cm^3

Consider two solid spheres A and B of the same size and $D = 5.5$ for each. Suppose A has a constant $D = 5.5$ throughout. Suppose B has an outer shell with constant $D = 4.5$ reaching halfway to the center, and a core with constant $D = 12.5$. Then A and B have the *same* mass and mean density.

Can we distinguish A and B? Yes. Sphere B rolls down an incline faster. This speed is related to its *moment of inertia*.

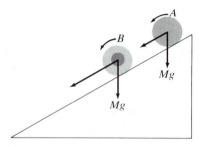

The moment of inertia I of a sphere is a measure of the concentration of mass toward the center: the smaller I is, the more concentrated is the mass.

For mass M and radius R, $I = zMR^2$
For a homogeneous sphere, $z = 0.4$
For a hollow sphere, $z = 0.67$

Thus, for sphere A, $z = 0.4$; for sphere B, we can calculate (see Exercise 44, Chapter 8) that $z = 0.34$.

For the Earth, from observations of the motions of artificial satellites and the Moon, $z = 0.3308$. Thus, like sphere B, the Earth has mass concentrated toward the center.

It is fascinating to follow how the realization grew that seismic waves carry crucial information on the way that the density changes within the Earth. Many of the perceptions are to the credit of K. E. Bullen, a New Zealander, who spent much of his working life in the University of Sydney, Australia (where he started my interest in the Earth's interior).

Let us begin the detective work on density by recalling that the speed of seismic waves depends on the physical properties of the rocks through which they travel, and that one of these properties is density. To be specific, we must refer to Box 2.2 and then to Box 7.2. There the algebra shows that the P and S velocities give the ratios: rigidity to density (μ/ρ) and incompressibility to density (k/ρ). The sad fact is that, because the elastic rock properties—rigidity and incompressibility—are unknown in the Earth, the seismic velocities *alone* cannot give us hard and fast density estimates. Nevertheless, because *changes* in elastic properties and density usually occur together and by similar amounts, changes in seismic speeds can be used as guides to changes in density.

Three examples immediately come to mind. When seismological research established the presence of sharp jumps in seismic velocities at the Moho, the mantle–core boundary, and the inner core boundary (see Figure 1.3), the overwhelming presumption was that density values also jump at these three boundaries. We would expect such density changes whether the sharp boundaries result from changes in the chemical composition of the rocks or in their physical character (as when water changes from liquid to ice).

By this argument, the great revolution brought to geophysical density studies by earthquake probes was to replace the continuous density increase in one or two arbitrary shells from the Earth's surface to its center assumed last century (see Chapter 1), by one with observationally-based major discontinuities at the top and bottom of the mantle and at the bottom of the liquid core. Beyond this conception, the new assumption was that, between the discontinuities, the curve of density increase with depth would follow in a general way the slopes of the velocity curves calculated from the P and S travel-time observations through the Earth (see Figure 7.3).

To be more quantitative about the density values at remote depths, further assumptions need to be introduced into arguments using seismic waves. Because these assumptions go outside of the study of earthquakes themselves, we put aside such developments here. Suffice it to say that among the most plausible and fruitful was the assumption that the whole of the Earth's liquid core is thoroughly mixed and homogeneous. And, perhaps less certainly, the same could be said for the lower mantle where velocity curves for P and S waves are smooth (see Figure 7.3). Homogeneous conditions (together with less sensitive assumptions on temperature) meant that the density increases in the lower mantle and liquid core could be calculated from the pure compression of the material in these shells by the enormous hydrostatic pressure at these depths. The classical equations whereby these calculations were first performed by the Americans, L. H. Adams and E. C. Williamson, in 1923, are given in Box 7.2. More realistic models of the Earth's density were subsequently constructed by K. E. Bullen, using more

Box 7.2   Calculation of Density in a Homogeneous Interior Region

In solid parts of the Earth, there is a relation between the density ρ and the moduli k and μ (see Box 2.2) on the one hand, and the P and S velocities α and β on the other:

$$\frac{\mu}{\rho} = \beta^2 \qquad (1)$$

and

$$\frac{k}{\rho} = \alpha^2 - \frac{4}{3}\beta^2 = \phi \qquad (2)$$

Here the Greek letter ϕ denotes the *seismic parameter*.

On the rather precise assumption of hydrostatic pressure p in the Earth, the increase in pressure dp, due to change in radius dr, is

$$dp = -\rho g \, dr \qquad (3)$$

where ρ and g are the density and gravitational attraction at radius r.

By definition, the incompressibility k is the ratio of the pressure change to the compression produced (assuming no change in heat or material), i.e.,

$$k = \rho \frac{dp}{d\rho} \qquad (4)$$

From (2), (3), and (4), we obtain

$$\frac{d\rho}{dr} = -\frac{\rho g}{\phi} \qquad (5)$$

This equation is named after the American physicists L. H. Adams and E. D. Williamson who in 1923 used it for the Earth.

But, from Box 1.1, the gravity at radius r is given by

$$g = Gm/r^2 \qquad (6)$$

where m is the Earth's mass inside radius r.

Equations (5) and (6) can be solved to give the density ρ as a function of r as long as ϕ is known from seismology.

precise seismological evidence. Needless to say, it would be better to figure the density values at depth by avoiding such assumptions as homogeneity used by these early workers. In the section following, the best modern approach is explained in which resonant vibrations of the whole Earth are used and the homogeneity assumption is relaxed.

What do the interior densities tell about composition? Obviously, we might simply compare the inferred densities with densities of known elements, compounds, minerals, and rocks and, from the closest matches, infer the chemical composition. There are two hitches. First, the temperatures and pressures in the Earth are *simultaneously* so large that so far it has not proved possible to measure in the laboratory densities of most likely candidates of rocks and minerals at conditions appropriate to the deep interior. Some ingenious comparisons, notably by Francis Birch of Harvard University, have been made between the observed seismic wave speeds and estimated densities for abundant elements. One such comparison is displayed in Figure 7.1 with the addition of curves for density versus the observed seismic parameter (ϕ in Box 7.2) for the Earth's mantle and core. The comparison indicates that the mantle curve falls near to the curves for aluminum and magnesium—consistent with a composition in the mantle of magnesium and aluminum oxides and silicates. By contrast, the curve for the core is drastically shifted into the region near the dense and abundant metal iron. This correlation is one strong reason why the liquid core is thought to consist of iron, perhaps alloyed with silicon or sulfur.*

Another remarkable inference on the core from the seismic velocities is that the inner core is solid. The argument, first put forward by K. E. Bullen in 1953, is ingenious and simple. The evidence is that the seismic P velocity α suddenly increases at the inner core boundary from 10.2 to 10.9 km/sec, or 6 percent. Thus, α^2 jumps by about 10 percent. But we know from equation (2) in Box 7.2 that α in a liquid (rigidity zero) depends directly upon the incompressibility modulus k, and inversely on the density ρ. Because it is virtually impossible at this great depth for density to *decrease* with increasing depth, the logic seems to

---

*Professor Birch commented in 1952: "Unwary readers should take warning that ordinary language undergoes modification to a high-pressure form when applied to the interior of the Earth; a few examples of equivalents follow:

High-pressure form:	*Ordinary meaning:*
certain	dubious
undoubtedly	perhaps
positive proof	vague suggestion
unanswerable argument	trivial objection
pure iron	uncertain mixture of all the elements"

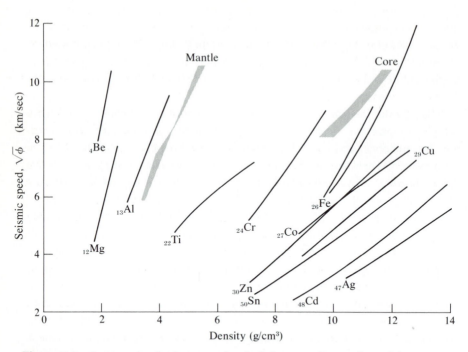

Figure 7.1 ϕ versus density for some chemical elements, the mantle, and the core. [Data largely from F. Birch, 1961.]

show that the increase in α^2 means a sudden increase of at least 10 percent in incompressibility. This contradicts separate physical evidence, however, that k changes very little in the extreme pressures of the core for plausible core materials. The contradiction can, fortunately, be simply resolved by assuming that the inner core, unlike the liquid outer core, has finite rigidity μ. We thus insert μ in the expression for α in Box 7.2 and figure its value if a contradiction is to be avoided. We obtain values of rigidity in the inner core similar to those in the Earth's lithosphere.

The alert reader will spot a fascinating implication. If the inner core is solid, S waves as well as P waves will travel through it. Therefore, observationally, we should encounter not only *PKIKP* waves, but also *PKJKP* waves, where J is a segment of S type in the inner core. For a number of reasons, including the high apparent damping of waves in the inner core (Box 6.2), the energy in *PKJKP* is likely to be two or three orders of magnitude less than that in *PKIKP*. Despite many special searches of seismograms, however, no unequivocal detection of this crucial core wave has yet been made although in 1972 B. Julian, D. Davies, and

R. Sheppard then at the Massachusetts Institute of Technology found some UEO's from LASA records that could be candidates. The search for *PKJKP* remains one of the great challenges in all of seismology.

Densities from Reflected Amplitudes

In Chapters 4 and 5, we looked at some beautiful reflections that were echoes of earthquake waves from sharp boundaries inside the Earth. Some of these reflections were from within the crust (Figure 4.2), some from the upper mantle (Figure 4.4), some from the outer boundary of the core (Figures 4.6 and 5.2), and some from the inner core boundary (Figure 4.9). We discussed how, like depth sounding at sea, times of travel of these waves allow us to estimate rather precisely the depth of the reflecting surfaces. Further, we saw that the down-and-back travel times put rather strict limits on the average speeds at which the *P* and *S* waves will travel through the crust, mantle, and core.

Even more, however, can be done with reflected waves if we consider more than just the travel-time observations. As might be expected, a comparison of the relative *amplitudes* of reflected earthquake waves can give us, with some plausible assumptions, valuable fresh information. In particular, amplitudes of reflected waves can yield an estimate for the density of the rocks at the top of the Earth's inner core.

After it had become clear, in 1968, that the 125 km seismological array LASA in Montana had detected *PKiKP* waves reflected at steep angles from the inner core boundary (see Chapter 4), I began to ponder the implications of these measurements. In particular, I had on my desk the sharp and clear seismograms (Figure 7.2(a)) from LASA of *PcP* and *PKiKP* waves from the underground nuclear explosion FAULTLESS in Nevada, only 11° away from LASA. I asked myself: what can be said about the physical difference between the outer and inner core from the measurements of the size of these reflected waves? An answer is suggested if we recall that the strength of a reflected sound or light wave from the interface between two liquids, for example, is strongly dependent on just how great is the difference in physical properties between the two liquids. If there is a marked mismatch, such as between air and water, the reflection will be strong; if there is a smaller mismatch, as between oil and water, the reflected energy will be smaller. In the same way, the amplitudes of seismic waves reflecting from an interface of the core, such as *PcP* waves or *PKiKP* waves (see Figure 7.2), will depend on the contrast of elastic properties including density. We must be careful, however, because unlike sound and light waves an incident wave of *P* type gives

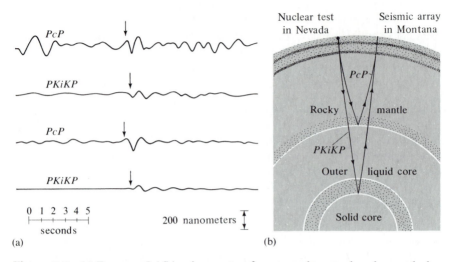

Figure 7.2 (a) Traces on LASA seismometers from an underground nuclear explosion in Nevada on January 19, 1968. Time proceeds from left to right. The vertical scale shows the magnitude of ground movement involved (200 nm is only half the wavelength of violet light). (b) *PcP* echoes from the outer core. These waves are the closest to a straight-down-and-back path yet reported. The angular distance between explosion and recording instruments was only 11°. *PKiKP* pulses represent echoes from the solid inner core. [From Bruce A. Bolt, "The Fine Structure of the Earth's Interior." Copyright © 1973 by Scientific American, Inc. All rights reserved.]

rise in a solid material to both reflected and refracted *P* and *SV* waves (see Box 2.1). Without writing the mathematical formulas down explicitly, it is evident that the amplitudes of reflected as well as refracted waves will be some function of the speeds of *P* and *S* waves and the density on each side of the boundary. In general, therefore, we will need already to know many parameters in order to obtain another if we are to use amplitude measurements.

There is a great simplification, however, when the seismic *P* ray through the mantle travels nearly vertically, as is the case for the *PcP* and *PKiKP* rays from FAULTLESS to LASA. The distance between the source and receiver is so small that the angle of incidence at the two boundaries of the core is less than 5 degrees. This means that incident *PcP* waves have very little motion in a direction along the surface of the mantle–core boundary and so produce little *S*-wave motion there. In any event because the outer core is liquid no *S* waves would penetrate shell E. Under these simplified circumstances, the reflection coefficient for the steep *PcP* waves at the mantle–core boundary is proportional to a term that depends only on the *P*-wave velocities on each side of the boundary and the densities on each side of the boundary. Similarly, the reflection coefficient at the inner core boundary does not depend upon the S-wave velocity (and hence, rigidity; see Box 2.2) which is zero in shell F and not known well in the inner core (shell G).

After some thought along these lines, I realized that if it was assumed that the reflection coefficient at the mantle–core boundary was approximately known from independent earlier studies (a reasonable proposition in 1970), the ratio of the observed amplitudes of the *PcP* wave to the *PKiKP* wave in Figure 7.2 should depend on the relative densities at each side of the *inner core* boundary.

To help matters, several other troublesome problems dropped out rather neatly. Because the *PcP* and *PKiKP* waves were recorded by the same seismographs at LASA, local effects due to the different ray paths under the recording stations disappeared, as did any effect of the recording seismographs themselves. Similarly, as is clear from Figure 7.2, the ray paths of *PcP* and *PKiKP* are almost identical in the mantle. Therefore, along the two legs in the mantle the waves attenuate the same amount from geometrical spreading, damping, and irregularities of mantle structure. We are then left with the two legs, corresponding to K, in the outer core. Because these are not compensated by companion *PcP* legs, some allowance has to be made for the decrease in amplitude suffered by *PKiKP* along its K legs because of the additional spreading of energy and damping in the core. The geometrical spreading is not in much doubt because it depends on the known speed of the P waves and the core geometry. Fortunately, also, the material of the outer core damps P waves of high frequencies very little. (This interesting result has already been discussed separately in Chapters 4 and 6.)

At this point we assume that we already know, from independent seismological inverse methods, values for P-wave velocities on each side of the inner core boundary. (Many estimates of these existed long before the *PKiKP* wave study— see Figure 7.5.) With this final assumption, the only parameter still unknown is the density ratio at the inner core boundary.

At this stage, I was joined in the work by A. Qamar. We first calculated a graph showing the change in ratio of amplitudes of *PKiKP* to amplitudes of *PcP* at the Earth's surface in terms of various density ratios at the inner core boundary. This computation gave a series of curves, one for each assumed value for attenuation in the core and for the assumed properties at the mantle–core boundary. Excitement grew as the final calculations drew to a finish. The most likely values, when compared with the observed amplitudes on Figure 7.2, gave a density ratio of about 0.87. This factor, when divided into the known density at the bottom of the outer core of 12.3 g/cm^3, yielded a density at the top of the inner core of 14.0 g/cm^3.

Was such a value plausible? First, it was well within the range of independent estimates made on broader arguments by other workers. For a number of reasons that need not detain us, the estimate of 14 g/cm^3 should be considered as an upper bound, yet, only a few years previously, central densities in the Earth as high as 18 g/cm^3 were seriously considered. Finally, such a density was in line with the results of "shock wave" experiments on iron made at laboratories specializing in very high-pressure experiments on materials. These laboratory experiments suggested that iron has a density close to 13 g/cm^3 at the great pressures at the center of the Earth.

It is gratifying indeed that, from simple measurements of seismograms in the laboratory, i.e., reading with a ruler the amplitudes of core waves shown in Figure 7.2, it is possible to say something about the density of rocks in the most remote part of the Earth. Rock from these depths will never be sampled and taken into the laboratory so that it can be weighed, yet earthquake probes can be found to satisfy our curiosity on its nature.

Densities from Earth's Resonant Vibrations

We foreshadowed in Chapter 6 that the measurements of periods of the vibrating Earth provide information on its interior physical properties. Just as the pitch of a tolling bell depends upon its elasticity and density, so after a great earthquake, the terrestrial bell tolls for geophysical knowledge.

The necessary procedures to infer density values through the Earth's interior, based upon the measured very long periods of the resonant T and S modes described in Chapter 6, were developed only after the heady successes of the early 1960's when the modes were initially recognized and measured. At first, the method of simple comparison between theoretical periods calculated for currently fashionable models and the observed periods of the eigenvibrations was used. Workers at the time had, in fact, every reason to be delighted that distributions of density and elastic parameters, constructed by independent methods (e.g., using travel times of short-period P and S waves), predicted periods that were within 1 percent or so of the observed periods. Clearly, we were on the right track.

Soon, however, demand sharpened for more precise values of interior density and other unknown parameters, and a host of competing new Earth models was launched on the geophysical ocean. Many of these efforts soon foundered, mainly because fresh great earthquakes, such as the gigantic Good Friday earthquake in

1964 in Alaska already mentioned, provided more extensive and sometimes more precise measurements of the pitch of the Earth's vibrations. As the 1970's progressed, more fundamental questions arose: what resolution of the interior mysteries could be ultimately achieved? And what precision and range of periods of eigenvibrations must be observed to provide optimum information? These basic conundrums are just those we discussed in Chapter 1 when we contrasted "direct" and "inverse" problems and, at this stage, it might be useful to reread the discussion given there with the present problem in mind.

Without using technicalities, we can give an elementary account of the procedures currently followed in refining the density curves inside the globe. The starting point is some available model of the Earth that we feel is a reasonable one. Such a model is defined in Figure 7.3 as three simple curves against depth of the three cardinal parameters: P velocity (α), S velocity (β) and density (ρ). This Earth model, called CAL6, was computed by my students and me at the University of California, Berkeley, in the late 1970's to take into account the seismological information then available. Notice that the shapes of the curves follow the main seismological features. In summary, there are some irregularities in the upper mantle (sympathetic to the Gutenberg "low-velocity layer" and discontinuities at 400 and 650 km), decreased velocities at the bottom of the mantle (region D″), and, of course, sharp jumps in velocities at the boundaries of the core.

The next step is to calculate theoretically the periods of T and S fundamental and overtone modes for the adopted model (in this example, for CAL6). We then subtract these from the values of the corresponding observations. Because CAL6 is not an exact replica of the Earth, we do not get a list of zeroes, but small numbers, called "residuals." These residuals are the keys to further progress, and the strategy that follows is to alter the adopted model CAL6 to make these residuals *as small as possible*.

One effort to make the differences between observation and predicted periods smaller is illustrated in Figure 7.4. Here, small offsets in the three curves for density and P and S speeds have been introduced (actually by a computer calculation) in order to improve the fit between observation and theory. Most of the trial offsets in Figure 7.4 are spiky and rather improbable (because they would give rise to reflected seismic waves that are not in fact observed). Yet, at least, they give an indication of the fidgeting around the initial model that is required to reduce the residuals to zero.

Many such revisions have been made in the last few years and continue at the time of writing. We will likely never see a *final* solution of the problem because new data are always coming along. At a certain stage, however, the fit will be

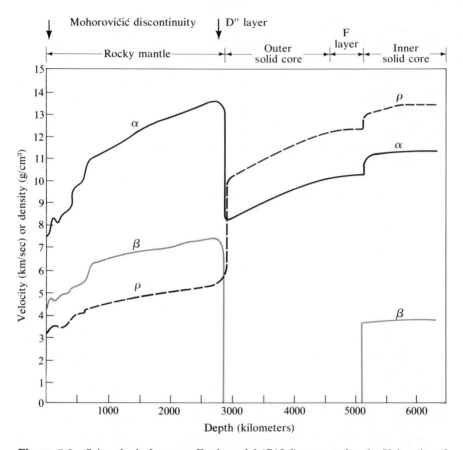

Figure 7.3 Seismological average Earth model (CAL6) computed at the University of California, Berkeley. The model, which took the seismological information available in 1978 into account, is defined by three curves. The curves show the variation in the Earth's density with depth, the average velocity of P waves (α), and the average velocity of S waves (β). Since S waves are not propagated through liquids, the β curve is interrupted by the Earth's outer core. The energy in an S wave, however, can be transmitted as a P wave through the liquid core and then reconverted into an S wave for transmission through the solid inner core.

close enough to make it worthwhile to adopt a reference Earth model, perhaps by international agreement. Physicists, chemists, and astronomers can then use this standard as a base for their own calculations. Tables 3, 4, and 5 of the Appendix list values of density and elastic parameters for a recently proposed reference model PREM, as well as corresponding values for CAL8, which is a

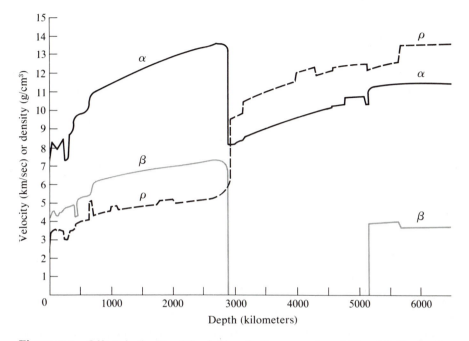

Figure 7.4   Offsets in the *P* and *S* seismic velocity curves (α and β) and in the density curve produced on a computer in an attempt to obtain a closer fit between observed resonant frequencies of the Earth and frequencies calculated from the starting model.

later (1981) improved version of CAL6. These models have become rather realistic with the incorporation of key structural details from earthquake probes and even the viscous properties that damp the eigenvibrations (see Box 6.2). The small differences between the listed values give one indication of the degree of uncertainty that still exists in the deep interior. Generally, the discrepancies are quite small.

Before leaving the density in the Earth, it is important to state just how the values in Figure 7.3 and Table 4 in the Appendix should be interpreted. It would be wrong to leave the impression that the density at any depth can be found just by reading off the value from the curve of Figure 7.3. Actually, by drawing such simple curves, we have been forced to misrepresent the situation. Let us reconsider. We have a finite number of observations of periods of resonant vibrations (these days about 500). Yet the density curve in Figure 7.3 is mapped out by an *infinite* number of points.

Put in this way, we can see that, given the finite number of observations, we can never determine every density point along the curve. By drawing smooth curves with a pen, we have produced average values over ranges of depth. It is such smoothed values that we list in Table 4 (Appendix) against a definite depth, whereas we should list them as average values within a shell of a certain thickness. The most recent work that a colleague, R. A. Uhrhammer, and I have done on CAL8 indicates that, in the Earth's liquid core, if we wish to estimate density values within 1 percent, we must regard the value as the average through a shell 250 km thick. Regarded in this light, all graphs and tables should carry a notice: **Warning: all point values may be dangerous to your work.** Of course, if we understand what the density curves represent, then we can proceed to use them with due caution.

Temperatures

How can we find out how hot the Earth is? Once again, the study of earthquake waves that have penetrated inner Earth can, when combined with laboratory experiments on the effects of heating rocks, tell us a good deal about the way temperature varies in the Earth. Considerable contributions on the relations between earthquake parameters, density, and temperature estimates have been made by Francis Birch of Harvard University and John Verhoogen of the University of California, Berkeley.

It was recognized last century that in mines and boreholes the temperature increases with depth. Yet, even with the deepest mines, we observe only the top few kilometers of the Earth, and we might be rightly skeptical about extrapolating the observed temperature increase far into the deep interior.

In recent years, a major experimental effort has been carried out by geophysicists to measure the amount of heat that is flowing through the surface rocks in many continental and oceanic areas. Now there are more than 5000 heat flow measurements from around the world, although the distribution is still uneven geographically. Heat flow is not measured directly, but in terms of the temperature gradient and the thermal conductivity of the rocks. Under the oceans, measurements are made by dropping a long, heavy cylinder into the soft sediments and measuring the temperatures at intervals along the cylinder with fixed electric thermometers. In the continents, boreholes are drilled into the rock (or mines are used) and thermometers are placed at various levels. The thermal conductivity of the rock is also required so that samples of sediments or rock are usually taken back to the laboratory for measurement.

Heat flow is usually high in volcanic and geothermal areas, and it decreases as the age of the ocean floor increases; there is also a decrease in heat flow with increasing age of geological provinces in continental areas. Usually observations of heat flow range from 20 to 120 milliwatts per square meter (see Appendix) with a global average of about 60 milliwatts,* and most heat flow values lie within 30 percent of the average value. While patterns of heat flow are different in continental and oceanic regions, the most frequently observed values are the same for oceans and continents, although the actual heat flow at any place may be masked by the circulation of water through the crustal rocks.

What are the sources of the Earth's heat that flows out and is lost in space? Two major sources that certainly play major roles are the store of heat left over from the early molten condition of the Earth and the heat that is produced by disintegration of radioactive elements within the rocks. If the amount of radioactive substances contained in common surface rocks, such as granite, is typical of the proportions inside the Earth, more heat would be generated by radioactive decay than is lost through the surface, and the temperature of the interior would increase and we would have a liquid rather than a solid mantle. (There is evidence to suggest, however, that radioactive materials are mainly concentrated in the rocks of the crust of the Earth.)

We can extrapolate downward into the Earth using these heat flow values, and assuming that the conduction properties of crustal rocks are known (including the amount of radioactive heat produced in the crust), we find that at the base of the crust at depths of 30 to 50 km the temperature is somewhere between 500 and 800°C. (The temperatures reached in blast furnaces and erupting magma are commonly between 1000 and 1500°C.) From this near-surface estimate, we must begin our journey inward and try to infer how temperature varies with depth.

First, it will help to say something about the way that heat can be transmitted. Frequently, we use such expressions as "heat flowing," "heat seeping," "temperatures being raised and lowered," to imply the transfer of heat energy from one location to another during a finite time. More precisely, the means by which the heat energy is transmitted are threefold: conduction, convection, and radiation. All these processes may occur deep within the planet, singly, or in various degrees of association.

Conduction is the most common means of heat transfer in nature. It is a process by which heat energy is transferred in heated material from the high-temperature parts to the cooler parts by a change in kinetic energy of the molecules. The materials of the Earth have different heat conductivities. Some solids, such as metals, are relatively good conductors of heat, whereas other solids, called insu-

---

*1.5×10^{-6} cal/cm^2/sec, in a common but older notation (see Table 1 in the Appendix).

lators, are relatively poor conductors. Conduction is typically a very slow process, whatever the precise thermal conductivity of the terrestrial material. In a body as large as the Earth, conduction through the whole interior must take many billions of years.

A much more efficient way of transporting heat from one place to another is by *convection*. In this mechanical process a bodily transfer of the heated material from one place to another occurs. It commonly occurs in liquids, through buoyant movements. Thus, in a saucepan of heated soup, the soup at the bottom expands, becomes less dense, and rises, forming an upward current toward the surface. There, cooling takes place into the air and the soup becomes denser and falls under gravity—forming convection cells. However, if the soup is thick, its viscous properties tend to prevent the upwelling of the buoyant liquid and the descent of the cold. When this happens, the soup may get hotter and hotter at the bottom of the saucepan until steam forms or it burns.

In the Earth, the only large parts that are liquid in the usual sense are the outer core and the oceans. Convection currents in the oceans are commonplace, and if the inferred temperature conditions and viscosities are correct, convection also occurs in the liquid core. In addition, there is indirect evidence that *slow* convection of the rocks (perhaps at a rate of a few centimeters per year) in the mantle takes place over long geological times. While in the short term, we can think of mantle and crustal rocks as solid and rigid—that is, S waves pass through them, it is the case that if the forces upon them are maintained for a very long time the rocks will flow. For example, on field trips geologists and archeologists can point to exposed rocks and ancient monuments that have been deformed by slow flow (but not fractured) under gravitational and tectonic forces. Unlike the soup analogy, rocks of the mantle are not only heated from below but they also contain radioactive sources of heat within them. The argument is therefore that over many geological epochs, buoyancy forces, due to the rock thermally expanding, produce a slow thermal convection. Some models of mantle flow have the convection cells extending from the top of the mantle down to the core boundary at depths of 2900 km; in other models, large-scale convection is confined typically to the outer 700 km of the mantle, which is the depth of the deepest earthquakes.

The third way to transmit heat from a source of high temperature to one of lower temperature involves no material transfer by either convection or conduction. Rather, heat energy is transmitted as *radiation,* such as the infrared heat waves that we feel coming from the sun. It turns out that temperatures in the Earth's deep interior are probably high enough that some heat is radiated from greater depths toward the cooler crust, but the proportion of the heat transferred in this way is less than that transferred by conduction and certainly less than that which can be transported by convection.

Let us now turn to the seismological evidence on temperature. Because earthquake shear waves propagate through the mantle, we can conclude that, apart from local areas (such as may occur near volcanoes), the rocks are not molten, at least in the short term. Much laboratory work has now been done on rocks at the range of high temperatures and pressures that occur in the *upper* mantle, and something is known about the effect of pressure on their melting temperature. Based on these temperatures and the seismic evidence of no large-scale melting, it seems unlikely that, at a depth of 100 km, the temperature would exceed 1200°C, or that, at the bottom of the mantle, the temperature is greater than about 5000°C (see Figure 7.5).

A little more speculation is possible in the upper mantle. In many regions, as has been discussed in earlier sections, the seismological evidence is that, at depths of about 80 km, the S velocity, and perhaps even the P velocity, decreases somewhat over a range of 50 to 100 km (see Figure 7.3). This "low-velocity layer" below the lithosphere coincides with the asthenosphere discussed in Chapter 4. One interpretation of this shell with its low S seismic velocities is that the temperture there is high enough to reduce the rigidity of the rocks. Perhaps the rocks are almost, but not quite, molten.

Some workers have endeavored to make inferences on the thickness of the lithosphere based on the idea of partial melting of the asthenosphere and the global measurements of heat flow. The argument is that the depth of the bottom of the lithosphere at any place can be determined from the depth at which the inferred temperature–depth curve intersects the calculated melting curve for the mantle rocks. When this correlation is made, it turns out that the inferred lithosphere is thinnest along the oceanic ridges where the thickness is only 5 kilometers or so. Interestingly, the correlation also indicates that the lithosphere increases in thickness to over 10 km under the oldest ocean basins and to several hundred kilometers under the old continental shields. All these estimates are at least reasonable and are in line with the seismological evidence on structure such as that discussed by Jordan (Chapter 5) from earthquake waves. If the bottom of the lithosphere indeed coincides with the depth of incipient melting, then the actual temperature is likely to be in the range of 900° to 1400°C. Under continents, a lithosphere of thickness 200 km would yield a temperature of about 1200°C at the bottom.

It is intriguing that this estimate has independent support from the properties of fragments of mantle rock that have been found in rock pipes called kimberlites

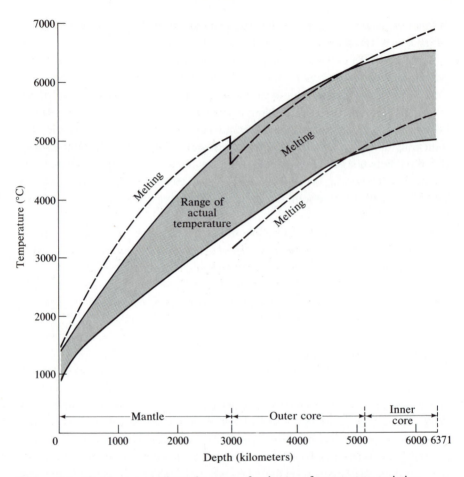

Figure 7.5   These curves indicate the range of estimates of temperature variation inside the Earth. At present the uncertainty is quite high. The consequences of adopting any particular estimate can be important in terms of the prediction of melting in the Earth.

in continental areas, such as in the Kimberley diamond-mining district of South Africa. These mantle fragments appear to have reached their equilibrium conditions at a pressure and temperature that corresponds to a depth of about 180 km and at a temperature of about 1200°C.

Figure 7.5 is a bold try at tracing the range of temperatures from the surface to the center. With the present uncertainties, it seems best to give a range of plausible values as outlined by the full black lines: the actual temperature at any depth is very likely to be somewhere between them. At the top of the mantle we have a narrow range near 1200°C and at the bottom of the mantle there is a spread between 3500 and 5000°C. The upper limit is constrained by the need to keep the actual temperature below the theoretical curve (shown as a dashed line) that gives the melting point at the given depth. The lower curve is harder to fix, but is suggested by a relatively low rate of temperature increase consistent with large convection cells through the mantle that efficiently carry the heat upward.

The curious boundary region D″ (see Figure 4.3) that was explored in Chapter 5 appears pregnant with information on heat changes in Earth. Any decrease in P and S velocities (see Figure 7.3) there can be accommodated by a trade-off between density and temperature of the rocks just above the core boundary. The form of the trade-off is set out quantitatively in equation (2) of Box 7.3. The balance between the various terms means that heavy elements like iron might be mixed in D″ into the ordinary mantle rocks to increase the density or there could be a rapid rise in temperature throughout the D″ shell to offset the effects of denser elements. There is always a tug-of-war between the parameters. Increased density through a change in composition will accommodate the decreased seismic wave speeds as will increased temperatures. Sorting out the separate effects of such changes is rather difficult, and all we can say is that the likely decreased seismic velocities in D″ may mean an extra few percent density increase or an extra few hundred degrees temperature rise (or perhaps a combination) compared with the normal increases higher in the mantle.

The Earth's core is so remote that only the most general arguments from basic physics can be used to estimate temperature. From the seismological observations (Chapter 4), the outer core is liquid and the inner core probably is solid. The boundary between the outer and inner core is sharp as we see from the *PKiKP* and *PKIIKP* reflections discussed earlier (Figures 4.9, 5.9, and 7.2). We also know from the amplitudes of core waves such as *PKKKKKKP* (see Figure 4.5) that the damping in the outer core is almost nil, while from core waves like *PKIKP* and *PKIIKP* (see Figure 4.9) damping in the inner core is very high. The suggestion is therefore that although the inner core is solid it is close to melting.

In the core portion of Figure 7.5, the dashed curves are plausible but largely speculative melting point curves for a material that is mainly iron. The upper full curve for temperature has been drawn to join on to the upper boundary temperature at the bottom of the mantle (5000°C) and to extend *above* the melting curve in the outer core and just below in the inner core. This curve predicts a (maximum) temperature at the Earth's center of 6500°C. The lower full curve in the core is also drawn to join smoothly onto the minimum plausible temperature curve in

---

Box 7.3   Changes from Homogeneous Conditions

In general the rocks in an interior shell of the Earth will change their properties by
  (a) changes in pressure p
  (b) changes in composition (inhomogeneity)
  (c) changes in temperature.
Thus equation (5) of Box 7.2 must be amended as done by B. A. Bolt in 1957.
Because, for (b) and (c), the right side does not equal the left side, put

$$\theta = -\frac{\phi}{\rho g}\frac{d\rho}{dr} \tag{1}$$

where θ is an *index of state*.
  When $\theta = 1$, conditions are homogeneous and adiabatic,
      $\theta > 1$, there is, generally, additional heavy material,
      $\theta < 1$, there is, generally, a sharp temperature increase or instability.
  K. E. Bullen showed in 1963 that

$$\theta = \eta - \frac{\alpha\tau\phi}{g} \tag{2}$$

where τ is the additional temperature gradient above adiabatic conditions, α is the coefficient of thermal expansion, and

$$\eta = g^{-1}\frac{d\phi}{dr} + \frac{dk}{dp} \qquad \text{(see Box 7.2)} \tag{3}$$

---

the mantle. In the inner core, it is somewhat controlled by calculations that assume optimistically that the density and pressure in the solid inner core (taken to be pure iron) are well known. Overall the range of temperatures indicated in Figure 7.5 is a fair indication of the various uncertainties.

Because at present it appears impossible to fix temperatures in the mantle to better than 500°C and in the core to better than 1000°C or so, we cannot be very sure about the chemical composition of inner Earth. Clearly, for comparative purposes much more work remains to be done on melting and physical conditions of rocks and iron alloys that are likely to occur at great depth. Progress also depends crucially on obtaining more precise seismological estimates of velocity and density because it turns out that at any depth it is the *rate of change* of the quantities that is critical rather than the average values.

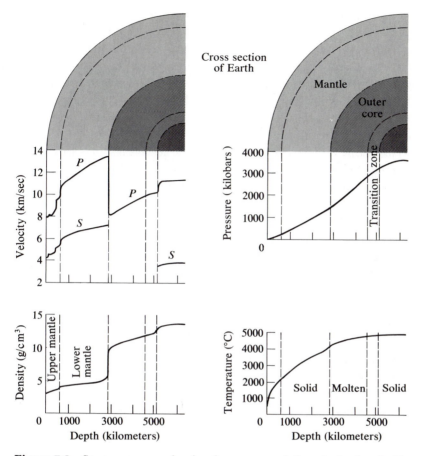

Figure 7.6 Summary curves showing the average variation of seismic velocities, density, pressure, and temperature inside the Earth.

Summary of the Earth's Cross Section

It is appropriate here to summarize the main physical properties inside the Earth that have emerged in the twentieth century. Much of the seismological synthesis has been brilliant, a lot of it has been accumulative and repetitious. A summary is given in Figure 7.6 in a simplified form. Remember, of course, that when a particular value for a shear wave velocity or pressure, for example, is read from Figure 7.6 at a particular depth in the Earth, the estimates are averages over a range of depths and that the total uncertainties are not adequately expressed by the lines drawn on the diagram. The full implications of this inferential problem, at once frustrating and challenging, were discussed in Chapter 1. Nevertheless, the summary graphs help in visualizing the marked changes in properties within our planet and, except perhaps for temperature, it is unlikely that future work will alter by more than 5 percent here and there any of the values given in the diagrams. More specific numerical values for two models of the seismic velocities and densities are given in Tables 3 and 4 in the Appendix, and values for gravity and pressure and elastic moduli are given in Tables 4 and 5.

This book has tried to convey the elegance of the achievement of seismologists from the time of R. D. Oldham to today in mapping out the interior of the Earth. In the preceding chapters, we have seen how, just in this century, specific measurements made on the Earth's surface have been converted into parameters on the inside of the Earth. The resulting terrestrial models give rather close estimates of the various physical properties such as density, pressure, and solidity at the center of the globe. They allow calculations to be made concerning the response of the Earth to the attraction of the Sun and Moon, the change in rates of the Earth's rotation, and the variations in the orbits of artificial satellites. In addition, we have seen how the work already done depends upon clever simplifications and plausible hypotheses and therefore leaves unresolved some basic questions.

Thus, at the end, the vista spread before us by Oldham in 1906 of using the seismograph to "see into the Earth as if we could drive a tunnel through it" still tugs at our imaginations. Although seismology is no longer in its infancy, but has achieved many triumphs, there is still need to probe further with finer instruments. *Caviat viator.*

Perry Byerly (1897–1978)
"For the seismographic stations in the eastern lee of the
Sierra Nevada, waves from coastal earthquakes are
blocked or much delayed. The most direct explanation
is a root of lighter rocks extending into the mantle."

CHAPTER 8

Exercises and Exposures

1. What was R. D. Oldham's seismological evidence that there is a distinct core to the Earth, based upon the upper and lower curves in the travel-time diagram in Box 1.2? By comparison with the modern travel-time curves in Box 3.2, show that the delayed observations along the upper curve (attributed by Oldham to *S* waves passing through the core) are actually the reflected waves *SS*, which lie entirely in the mantle.

2. Consider the deflection of a plumb bob at distance 1 km away by the Great Pyramid (Box 1.1). The pyramid's mass is estimated to be 5×10^9 kg. By substituting in equation (4) of Box 1.1, calculate the angle of deflection θ. Does it therefore seem experimentally feasible to use Cheops to measure the mass of the Earth?

3. Suppose in equation (4) of Box 1.3 the gradient p of the travel-time curve remained constant for a range of distances Δ. Could you integrate (4) in this range, and what is the implication for the corresponding velocity V as a function of r?

4. Consider the way that the wave motions in surface Love waves decrease with depth in the Earth (Box 2.4). Would an earthquake with focus at depth 110 km produce (compared with the fundamental mode) significant first-higher mode Love waves with period 30 sec? At what depths would there be little second-higher mode energy in Love waves of 30 sec period?

5. Write the equation for a progressive surface seismic wave moving along the negative *x*-axis with the following characteristics: amplitude, 0.5 cm; period 2 sec; wavelength, 50 cm (Box 1.5).

6. When a note in the middle of a piano keyboard is struck vigorously and then, on lifting the finger, the sustaining pedal is immediately depressed, the same tone persists. Explain this. Does a great earthquake cause the same effect for the Earth's resonant vibrations?

7. The fundamental frequency of an open organ pipe 100 cm long is 180 vibrations/sec. What is the velocity of sound in the pipe? What is the frequency of the second possible overtone of that open pipe? Make a diagram showing the loops and nodes in this problem. What is the analogy in the Earth?

8. A wire 1 m long has a mass m of 0.010 kg per meter and is under a tension F of 10 kg. If the wire is rigidly held at both ends and is set into vibration, find the frequencies of the fundamental and first two overtones (Box 6.1). [Hint: The velocity of a wave in the string is $\sqrt{F/m}$.]

9. Why does a pool of clear water appear shallower than it really is (Box 2.1), and why does the apparent depth of water in a tank change with the position of the observer? What is the analogous problem in seismic prospecting of Earth structure?

10. What kind of image would a spherical lens give of a point source of light? A large piece of glass is in the form of a sphere of radius 8 cm. A point source of light is placed on the surface of the sphere. If the index of refraction of the glass is 1.6, locate the image of the point source (Box 2.1). From this exercise, deduce what the image of a deep earthquake source would be on the other side of the Earth.

11. Water has an index of refraction of 1.33. At what angle must a beam of light strike the water surface in order that the reflected beam may be plane-polarized (Chapter 2)? Could the same effect occur when a beam of seismic S waves strikes the Mohorovičić discontinuity? [Hint: The tangent of the angle of incidence for complete polarization equals the refractive index of the reflector.]

12. A deep-focus earthquake occurred near the Tonga Islands and good readings of pP waves as well as P waves were observed at the following stations:

Station	Distance away ($\Delta°$)	$pP - P$ time
Berkeley	65°	65 sec
Tucson	80°	67 sec
St. Louis	90°	70 sec

Using ray diagrams and the velocity distribution given in Table 3 in the Appendix, make an estimate of the depth of focus of the earthquake from the $pP - P$ interval.

13. The motion of particles of rock during the passage of Rayleigh waves is, in general, retrograde elliptical. Draw small elliptical orbits at a number of depths illustrating this motion. How do these orbits compare with the motion of water particles as a water wave passes by?

14. Confirm the distance of the earthquake recorded in Figure 3.4 (by means of the time-distance curve, Box 3.2), and deduce the origin time of the earthquake.

15. The University of California seismograph array centered at Berkeley records the P wave from a distant earthquake as it moves across the array with an azimuth of 20° west of north. The time interval dT between the arrival times of the wave at stations $d\Delta = 100$ km apart is 8 sec. Estimate (using $dT/d\Delta$ and the time curve in Box 3.2) the approximate distance of the source away from Berkeley.

16. In a continental area, the crust is believed to consist of an upper layer of thickness 15 km and P-wave velocity 6.0 km/sec, overlying a lower layer of thickness 10 km and P-wave velocity 7.0 km/sec. The upper-mantle P-wave velocity is 8.0 km/sec. Calculate arrival-time curves for refracted arrivals from a surface explosion and show whether or not the critically refracted P wave along the boundary between the crustal layers can be expected as a first arrival (Box 2.1). What are the distances from the source for seismographs to be placed if critical-angle reflections from the interfaces are to be observed? Finally, estimate the total length of the line of seismographs that would be required to define the upper mantle velocity to within 0.05 km/sec on the basis of first arrivals, if times can be read to 0.01 sec and distances are known with negligible error.

17. Free oscillations of a sphere are to be demonstrated in a laboratory class. A steel sphere, 20 cm in diameter, is available, and the Young's modulus for steel is 20×10^{11} dynes/cm^2. Assuming that Poisson's ratio is 1/3, compute the frequency of the first radial spheroidal oscillations ($_0S_0$). How would you excite and observe these oscillations? [Hint: The equation for the frequencies ω is $xR/\tan xR = 1 - x^2R^2\alpha^2/4\beta^2$, where $x = \omega/\alpha$, R is the radius, α and β are the P and S velocities, and Poisson's ratio is $\frac{1}{2}(\alpha^2 - 2\beta^2)/(\alpha^2 - \beta^2)$.]

18. At $\Delta = 60°$, the ray PcP has a travel time of 10 min 56.6 sec and a ray parameter $dT/d\Delta = 4.0$ sec/deg (see Box 2.3). The PKP ray with the same parameter travels to a distance of $\Delta = 148°$ with a time of 19 min 52 sec. Calculate how long it has taken the PKP ray to pass through the core and the travel times and distances of emergence at the surface of the corresponding $PKKP$ and $PKKKP$ rays (i.e., with the same $dT/d\Delta$).

19. Consider the seismic waves identified on the seismogram of Figure 3.4. Draw the corresponding rays roughly to scale, in a circle representing the Earth.

The *SKS* wave arrives before the direct *S* at this distance ($\Delta = 102°$). Explain how this is possible. The *SSS* wave has a larger amplitude on the seismogram than the *SS* waves. How can this be? There are no Love waves marked on the record, yet there are multiple *S* phases. Explain why this is possible.

20. You wish to determine the depth to the water table before drilling a well. Using small explosions and seismographs, you find that the *P*-wave velocity in the surface sediment is 600 m/sec and the velocity in the subsurface layer, presumably the water table, is 1500 m/sec. The intercept time, *T*, is 0.8 second. How deep is the water table (Box 2.1)?

21. Mars is Earth's neighbor, yet the two planets are radically different in many geophysical properties. Describe these differences and hazard a guess as to why they exist.

22. What is the strongest evidence at present for the presence of a *liquid* core inside the Earth? Explain, with reference to Figure 8.1, how diffracted seismic waves are generated by the core so that the core shadow is not total.

23. Show that if the mass, radius, and mean density of a planet are *M*, *R*, and ρ, respectively, that the central pressure P_c is

$$P_c \le \frac{3}{8\pi} \frac{GM^2}{R^4} \left(\frac{\rho_c}{\rho}\right)^{4/3}$$

where the density never decreases with depth and ρ_c is the central density. For the Moon, $M = 7.345 \times 10^{25}$ g, $R = 1738$ km, $\rho = 3.34$ g/cm^3. Using the above equation, estimate a *minimum* central pressure for the Moon.

24. The moment of inertia of the Earth (assumed symmetrical about its center) is $0.331 Ma^2$, where the mass *M* is 5.98×10^{27} g, and the radius *a* is 6370 km. If the Earth consists of a distinct core of radius 3470 km surrounded by a mantle of thickness 2900 km, and assuming the densities of the mantle and core to be uniform, find these densities (see Exercise 44).

25. Calculate the pressure required to reduce the volume of an iron specimen by 1 percent. (The bulk modulus for iron is 1.67×10^{12} dynes/cm^2.)

26. Given the bulk modulus and rigidity modulus of a rock as 2×10^{11} dynes/cm^2 and the density as 2.5 g/cm^3, find the velocity of longitudinal and transverse waves and Poisson's ratio (Box 2.2 and Exercise 17).

27. The coffee cup experiment. The radius of a spherical white coffee cup is 5 cm. A light source is located 50 cm from the cup at a height a little above the surface of coffee in the cup. Vary the position of the light source to

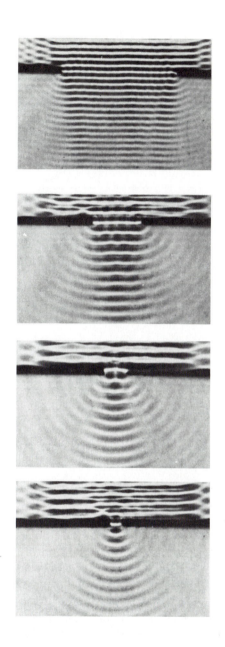

Figure 8.1 Ripples diffracted into quiet water by an opening.

produce a pattern of intense reflected light on the surface of the coffee (a *caustic* surface). Draw a diagram of the setup with several rays parallel to the line of symmetry (see Figure 8.2) and hence describe the formation of a caustic surface. What is the analogy with the *PKP* caustic at about 140° distance?

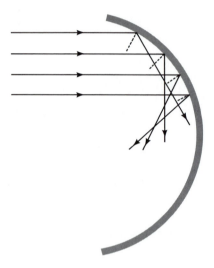

Figure 8.2   Ray reflection at a circular surface.

28. Consider, as an approximation, *P* rays in an Earth of uniform velocity, radius *r* and center *O*. Consider a source *F* on a diameter such that $OF = \frac{1}{10} r$. Consider stationary travel paths of *PP* type from *F* to a receiving station *R* on the surface, such that *FOR* is 90° (see Figure 2.2). Prove that three paths are possible (i.e., *pP*, *PP*, and *P'P'* types) in theory, such that the angle of incidence *i* at *S* is given by a cubic equation in i. [Hint: Use the sine rule and Snell's rule.]

29. Given that in the Earth there is a discontinuous decrease in the *P* velocity at the mantle–core boundary and a discontinuous increase in the *P* velocity at the outer-core–inner-core boundary, would you expect large, normal, or small amplitudes to be observed on seismograms for the following waves and distances: (a) *P* at 110°, (b) *PKP* at 140°, (c) *PKIKP* at 110°, (d) *PKIKP* at 140°, and (e) *PKIKP* at 180°?

30. Figure 7.6 shows increases of pressure, temperature, and density from the Earth's surface to the center. Of the three graph curves, which one is probably the most speculative and uncertain? Explain. How would you go about making a rough calculation of the confining pressure at the center of the Earth, using an average Earth density of 5.5 g/cm^3? What is the basic source of information on the value of density at various depths in the Earth? Specifically, what clue might exist that there is a sudden jump in density at a depth of about 2900 km?

31. A coiled spring such as that sold under the trade name "Slinky" can be used to demonstrate the distinction between P and S waves. Stretch this spring out gently on a smooth hard floor. Manipulate the spring at one end with a rhythmic motion that propagates a wave toward the other end of the spring. Can you produce both P and S motions simultaneously?

32. Could a seismograph capable of recording three components of motion on a ship at sea detect an earthquake? Could it be used to infer the earthquake position from the wave types recorded?

33. Why are at least three seismographic stations required to locate uniquely earthquake epicenters on the basis of P-wave arrival times?

34. For paths across the oceans, distinctive long-period Love waves ($T > 20$ sec) concentrated in a short time interval, corresponding to a velocity of about 4.4 km/sec, are observed on seismograms from horizontal component seismographs. Explain this in terms of the dispersion curves in Box 2.4. Would the Love wave train look the same for continental paths?

35. By scaling from the seismograph response curves of Box 3.1, estimate the wave amplitude of a 5 sec P wave as recorded on the BKS (Berkeley station) Sprengnether (15 sec) instrument if the BKS Wood-Anderson instrument showed a P-wave amplitude of 2 mm at 5 sec period.

36. Compare the arrival times of identified seismic waves on Figure 3.4 against the theoretical travel times in Box 3.2 ($\Delta = 90°$). Can you identify any other likely types of waves such as PPP?

37. At an epicentral distance of 153°, the travel time of the PKP wave is 20 min 10.0 sec and the gradient $dT/d\Delta$ (i.e., p, see Box 2.3) is 4.2 sec/deg. For the same ray parameter p, the travel time of PcP is 11 min 30 sec to a distance of 68°. Sketch these two rays from a surface focus in the Earth and also the ray $PKKP$ with the same ray parameter. Calculate from the property for p given in Box 2.3 that the travel time of this $PKKP$ wave is 28 min 50 sec at $\Delta = 237°$.

38. Consider a simple Earth model, similar to that used by Inge Lehmann (Box 1.4) with a mantle of depth 2900 km and constant P velocity 11 km/sec and a constant outer core velocity of 9 km/sec. Sketch, using Snell's law (Box

2.1) at the core boundary, the (straight line) rays for the core wave *PKP* that comes to the surface at $\Delta = 170°$ and $160°$. Show that, in fact, there are *two* *PKP* rays that can be drawn to each of these distances. What is the approximate minimum distance for which only one ray can be drawn (the *caustic point*)?

39. By considering the Lehmann Earth model above, show by a sketch that there is an outer shell of the Earth's core in which no straight line *PKP* ray (i.e., a chord) can be drawn. What is the depth in the core corresponding to the bottom of the shell in which no *PKP* ray bottoms?

   Repeat the geometrical construction for *SKS* rays assuming an average constant *S* velocity in the mantle of 6 km/sec. Show that in this case there is no shell at the top of the core in which *SKS* rays do not bottom.

40. The velocity of *P* waves in the inner core is known to jump to a value 6 percent greater than the velocity of *P* waves in the liquid outer core. Since $\alpha = \sqrt{(k + 4\mu/3)/\rho}$ and $\mu = 0$ in the outer core (see Box 2.2), give an argument why a plausible way to account for this jump in α is to give μ a finite value in the inner core. Hence, estimate the upper value for average μ and shear velocity in this solid inner core (use approximate values for *k* and ρ in Tables 4 and 5 in the Appendix.)

41. Calculate approximately the pressure at the center of a Moon model such as that given in Figure 4.11. Then, by a simple correlation with pressure in the Earth given in Figure 7.6, write down the corresponding *P* and *S* velocities and the density at the Moon's center.

   What is the main physical objection to such a simple prediction? Is the objection as strong for the prediction of interior properties of Mars?

42. Consider the free oscillations of the Earth described geometrically in Box 6.1. Sketch as in Figure 6.3 the surface pattern of nodal lines and displacements for the modes $_0T_3$, $_1T_4$, and $_0S_4$. Draw the internal nodal pattern for $_2S_0$, $_2S_2$, and $_2T_2$.

   Can properties of the inner core be inferred from frequency measurements of the modes $_0T_2$, $_1T_2$, $_0S_{40}$?

43. Because the Earth's free oscillations are damped, their amplitudes will slowly decrease with time after a great earthquake. Calculate (see Box 6.2) by what percentage the amplitudes of $_0T_2$, $_0S_2$, and $_0S_0$ have decreased after 20 hours.

44. The average mass and moment of inertia were given for a simple Earth model (sphere B) in Box 7.1. Verify by calculation from elementary mechanics the given moment of inertia and also that the masses of Model A and Model B are the same. [Hint: If *m* is the mass inside a sphere, moment of inertia *I*, radius *r*, and variable density $\rho(r)$,

$$m = 4\pi \int \rho r^2 \, dr$$

and

$$I = \frac{8}{3}\pi \int \rho r^4 \, dr \, .]$$

45. A relatively straightforward way of inferring which shells in the Earth's interior have relatively large changes in material properties is to calculate the homogeneity index θ (Box 7.3).

    In region D″ at the bottom of the mantle, the seismic velocities essentially do not change with depth. Show from the equations in Box 7.3 that this suggests either rapid temperature increases there or mixing in of heavier minerals or both.

    Why does a significant decrease in P velocity with depth in shell F in the core seem unlikely? [Hint: Assume $dk/dp \approx 3.0$ in D″ and F.]

46. Mathematical textbooks sometimes include a problem about the time it would take an object to travel (with no friction) through a hole bored in the Earth from the North Pole to the South Pole. The usual assumption is that the acceleration of gravity g at every point along the hole is proportional to the radius r. Indicate why this problem can have no relation whatever to planet Earth (see Table 4 in the Appendix).

47. In the above problem, let G be the gravitational constant, m be the mass contained in a sphere of the Earth of radius r, and σ be the mean density of matter inside this sphere. Let ρ be the density at distance r from the center. Then

$$g = Gm/r^2$$

and

$$m = 4\pi r^3 \sigma/3$$

Show that

$$\frac{dg}{dr} = 4\pi G (\rho - 2\sigma/3)$$

and hence that for realistic densities (see Table 4 in the Appendix) in the upper part of the Earth the gravity actually increases with depth.

48. Consider the properties of the viscoelastic material called Silly Putty. By dropping a ball of it, verify that it will readily bounce (and is thus elastic), yet if the ball is allowed to stand for a few hours on a surface it will flow into a flat disk (and is thus viscous). Will Silly Putty transmit both P and S waves? What will happen to their amplitude as they travel?

    By measuring the height h of 2 or 3 ($= n$) successive bounces of a golfball-sized sphere of Silly Putty, estimate (see Box 6.2) its damping decay constant β [where $h = h_0 \exp(-\beta n)$; $h_0 = $ initial height]. Hence estimate its Q value ($\beta = \pi f/Q$) for a frequency of 100 Hz.

Why would a large sphere of this material not make a satisfactory proto-type for the rocky material in the Earth's mantle so that the Earth's free vibrations (Chapter 5) could be modeled in the laboratory?

49. In another application of epicenter location by the Berkeley array (see Question 15), the incoming P waves were found to be approached from S20°E. The waves had an (apparent) surface velocity of 9.0 km/sec. The "true" velocity of P waves through the crust under the array is 6.0 km/sec. Estimate (see Box 2.1) the geographic location of the earthquake epicenter.

50. With the geometrical properties of types of seismic waves in mind (see Chapter 2), explain

(a) why the horizontally polarized S wave (SH) is observed at distances considerably greater than 105°, i.e., in the shadow of the Earth's core, yet the companion vertically polarized (SV) wave is not seen there.

(b) why multiple reflections of core waves like $PKKKKKP$ do not soon lose all their energy into refracted waves at the points of reflection.

(c) in what way the above observations strengthen the inference that the outer core is liquid.

Answers

1. Delay in travel-time curves (Box 1.2) at 120°   2. 2×10^{-6} degrees. No.

3. Constant velocity zone   4. No. About 100 km, 220 km, and below 600 km

5. $y = 0.5 \sin 2\pi \left(\dfrac{t}{2} + \dfrac{x}{50} \right)$ 7. 360 m/sec. 540 vibrations/sec

8. Fundamental 49.5 Hz; overtones 99 Hz, 148.5 Hz

10. Source on left side. Focus blurred, 26 cm to the left of the source. For earthquakes, focus is in interior of Earth on the right side, in line with the source and the center.

11. 53°.06   12. 290 km   14. 110°, 12 hr 41 min 40 sec

15. 30°   16. Yes. 50 km, 70 km, 12.8 km   17. 8.5×10^4 Hz

18. 8 min 55.4 sec. 28 min 47.4 sec, 236°   20. 262 m

22. Measurements of tides and free oscillations

23. 4.71×10^{10} dynes/cm^2 24. 12.55 g/cm^3, 4.17 g/cm^3

25. 1.67×10^{10} dynes/cm^2

26. $\alpha = 4.3$ km/sec, $\beta = 2.8$ km/sec, $\sigma = .13$

29. (a) small (b) large (c) small (d) small (e) large

32. Yes. Only from differential times of P-type waves   35. 38 mm

38. 152°   40. 2.0×10^{12} dynes/cm^2, 4.2 km/sec   41. Variation in rock types. No.

42. Yes. Yes. No.   43. 22%, 11%, 4%   45. θ would be negative in F.

48. Yes, S decays faster than P. The surface of the Earth would be flat in a very short time.   49. 19° away. Gulf of California

Appendix

Table 1   Geophysical units.

| | SI [rationalized mks] units and cgs units | |
	SI unit	Equivalent in cgs
Mass	1 kilogram [kg]	10^3 grams [g or gm]
Length	1 meter [m]	10^2 centimeters [cm]
Time	1 second [s or sec]	1 sec
Force	1 newton [N]	10^5 dynes
Pressure and elastic moduli	1 pascal [Pa] $\equiv$ 1 N m^{-2}	10 dyne cm^{-2}
Energy	1 joule [J]	10^7 ergs
Density	1 kg m^{-3}	10^3 g cm^{-3}
Power	1 watt [W]	10^7 erg sec^{-1}
Frequency	1 hertz [Hz]	1 cycle sec^{-1}

Common conversions	
1 meter	= 39.37 inches
	= 10^9 nanometers
1 statute mile	= 1609 m
1 pound [lb]	= 0.4536 kg
1 tonne	= 1000 kg
1 year	= 3.15567 $\times$ 10^7 sec
1 kg wt	= 9.807 N = 9.807 $\times$ 10^5 dynes
1 atmosphere of pressure [supports 0.76 m of mercury]	= 1.013 bar = 1.013 $\times$ 10^5 Pa
1 bar [10^6 dyne cm^{-2}]	= 10^5 Pa
1 calorie	= 4.184 J
1 heat flux unit [1 μ cal cm^{-2} sec^{-1}]	= 4.184 $\times$ 10^{-2} W m^{-2}
1 gal [1 cm sec^{-2}]	= 10^{-2} m sec^{-2}
1 meter per second [m sec^{-1}]	= 3.281 feet per second [ft sec^{-1}]
1 micro unit [μ]	= 10^{-6} m
0 Kelvin [K]	= $-273°$ Celsius [°C]

Table 2   Dimensions of the Earth (in SI units).

Equatorial radius	6.378149×10^6 m
Polar radius	6.35675×10^6 m
Volume	1.083×10^{21} m^3
Radius of sphere of equal volume	6.3708×10^6 m
Flattening (ellipticity)	1/298.256
Surface areas	
Land	$1.48 = 10^{14}$ m^2
Sea	3.62×10^{14} m^2
Mass	5.973×10^{24} kg
Gravitational const. × mass [including atmosphere]	3.986005×10^{14} m^3 sec^{-2}
Mean density	5.515×10^3 kg m^{-3}
Moments of inertia	
About polar axis	8.0378×10^{37} kg m^2
About equatorial axis	8.0115×10^{37} kg m^2
Core	0.920×10^{37} kg m^2
Coefficient of moment of inertia	0.33076
Sidereal day (rotation of Earth)	86,164 sec
Rotational angular velocity	7.292115×10^{-5} sec^{-1}
Equatorial gravity	9.780317 m sec^{-2}
Total geothermal flow	$[3.14 \pm 0.17] \times 10^{13}$ W
Mean surface heat flow	$[6.15 \pm 0.34] \times 10^{-2}$ W m^{-2}
Mass of atmosphere	5.1×10^{18} kg
Mass of oceans	1.4×10^{21} kg
Mass of crust	2.6×10^{22} kg
Mass of mantle	4.0×10^{24} kg
Mass of outer core	1.85×10^{24} kg
Mass of inner core	9.7×10^{22} kg
Mass of Moon	7.345×10^{22} kg
Radius of sphere of equal volume to Moon	1.738×10^6 m
Moon's coefficient of moment of inertia	0.391
Ratio $\dfrac{\text{mass of Earth}}{\text{mass of Moon}}$	81.302

Table 3 *P*-wave velocity (α) and *S*-wave velocity (β) at various depths. (The first column (I) is for Earth Model CAL8 and the second (II) for PREM* (see text).)

Depth (km)	α (km/sec) I	α (km/sec) II	β (km/sec) I	β (km/sec) II
0–10	4.30	—	2.30	—
10–20	7.50	—	4.30	—
20	7.96	8.11	4.52	4.49
40	7.97	8.10	4.45	4.48
80	8.00	8.08	4.36	4.67
150	8.08	8.03	4.36	4.44
220	8.23	7.99	4.48	4.42
220	8.23	8.56	4.48	4.64
300	8.51	8.69	4.68	4.70
400	9.08	8.91	4.89	4.77
400	9.41	9.13	5.09	4.93
500	9.72	9.65	5.26	5.22
600	9.97	10.16	5.42	5.52
640	10.20	10.22	5.51	5.55
640	10.20	10.22	5.70	5.55
670	10.68	10.27	5.85	5.57
670	10.68	10.75	5.85	5.95
800	11.10	11.11	6.26	6.26
1000	11.48	11.46	6.44	6.40
1200	11.78	11.78	6.54	6.52
1400	12.06	12.06	6.64	6.63
1600	12.32	12.33	6.75	6.74
2000	12.80	12.82	6.96	6.93
2400	13.26	13.28	7.12	7.11
2700	13.61	13.62	7.19	7.24
2780	13.67	13.69	7.17	7.26
2850	13.54	13.71	7.07	7.26
2885	13.37	13.72	6.96	7.26
2885	8.09	8.06	0	0
3000	8.27	8.25	0	0
3200	8.56	8.56	0	0
3400	8.84	8.83	0	0
3800	9.33	9.31	0	0
4200	9.74	9.69	0	0
4550	10.00	9.97	0	0
4800	10.12	10.14	0	0
5000	10.18	10.27	0	0
5155	10.19	10.36	0	0
5155	10.89	11.03	3.49	3.50
5200	10.94	11.05	3.50	3.52
5400	11.13	11.11	3.55	3.56
5600	11.24	11.17	3.58	3.60
6200	11.33	11.26	3.60	3.66
6371	11.33	11.26	3.60	3.67

*From "Preliminary Reference Earth Model" by A. M. Dziewonski and D. L. Anderson, *Physics of the Earth and Planetary Physics 25*, 297–356; 1981.

Table 4 Density and gravity at various depths. (The first column (I) is for Earth Model CAL8 and the second (II) for PREM (see text).)

Depth (km)	Density (g/cm^3) I	Density (g/cm^3) II	Gravity (cm/sec^2) I	Gravity (cm/sec^2) II
0–10	2.16	2.6*	982	982
10–20	3.26	2.90	983	983
20	3.34	3.38	984	984
40	3.35	3.38	985	984
80	3.36	3.37	986	985
150	3.40	3.37	988	988
220	3.41	3.36	991	990
220	3.42	3.44	991	990
300	3.47	3.48	994	993
400	3.58	3.54	998	997
400	3.64	3.72	998	997
500	3.84	3.85	1000	999
600	4.98	3.98	1002	1000
640	4.02	3.98	1002	1001
640	4.16	3.98	1002	1001
670	4.22	3.99	1002	1001
670	4.22	4.38	1002	1001
800	4.43	4.46	1001	999
1000	4.61	4.58	997	997
1200	4.74	4.69	994	994
1400	4.83	4.81	992	993
1600	4.92	4.91	992	993
2000	5.06	5.12	999	999
2400	5.23	5.32	1020	1018
2700	5.43	5.47	1048	1043
2780	5.52	5.51	1058	1053
2850	5.74	5.56	1066	1065
2885	5.92	5.57	1071	1068
2885	9.82	9.90	1071	1068
3000	10.01	10.07	1046	1044
3200	10.33	10.37	1001	998
3400	10.62	10.54	953	948
3800	11.11	11.11	848	842
4200	11.52	11.51	736	728
4550	11.84	11.79	634	623
4800	12.03	11.97	560	547
5000	12.14	12.09	502	485
5155	12.17	12.17	459	440
5155	13.34	12.76	459	440
5200	13.38	12.79	442	422
5400	13.49	12.88	368	352
5600	13.55	12.96	294	280
6200	13.59	13.08	76	63
6371	13.58	13.09	0	0

*Densities in the crust depend on whether oceans, continents, or a composite crust is being modeled.

Table 5 Pressure and elastic moduli at various depths. (The first column (I) is for Earth Model CAL8 and the second (II) for PREM (see text).)

Depth (km)	Pressure (kbars)		Rigidity, μ (kbars)		Incompressibility, k (kbars)	
	I	II	I	II	I	II
0	0	0		0		
20	5	6	682	441	1206	1315
80	25	25	639	674	1299	1303
150	48	48	645	665	1356	1287
220	72	71	686	656	1401	1270
220	72	71	686	741	1401	1529
300	99	99	760	769	1500	1618
400	135	134	856	806	1810	1735
400	135	134	921	906	1995	1899
500	172	171	1062	1051	2211	2181
600	211	210	1169	1210	2397	2489
640	227	226	1220	1226	2555	2528
640	227	226	1352	1226	2819	2528
670	239	238	1442	1239	2887	2556
670	239	238	1442	1548	2887	2999
800	296	296	1736	1749	3144	3182
1000	389	386	1912	1874	3526	3519
1200	482	478	2027	1996	3874	3850
1400	577	573	2130	2115	4186	4174
1600	673	669	2242	2232	4479	4494
2000	872	869	2451	2462	5022	5132
2400	1079	1080	2615	2692	5661	5794
2700	1244	1241	2807	2868	6315	6318
2780	1290	1293	2838	2909	6531	6449
2850	1332	1334	2862	2925	6697	6507
2885	1353	1358	2868	2938	6759	6556
2885	1353	1358	0	0	6427	6441
3000	1474	1472	0	0	6846	6581
3200	1683	1681	0	0	7569	7589
3400	1887	1886	0	0	8299	8303
3800	2279	2275	0	0	9671	9633
4200	2638	2631	0	0	10929	10814
4550	2918	2907	0	0	11840	11726
4800	3097	3180	0	0	12320	12306
5000	3225	3204	0	0	12581	12740
5155	3315	3289	0	0	12637	13047
5155	3315	3289	1625	1567	13654	13434
5200	3342	3316	1639	1582	13828	13498
5400	3451	3415	1700	1637	14444	13731
5600	3541	3497	1737	1681	14803	13922
6200	3689	3631	1761	1756	15097	14236
6371	3699	3639	1760	1761	15086	14253

Table 6   Seismic wave notation.

Symbol	Meaning
P	Primary wave
S	Secondary wave
K	*P* wave through outer core
I	*P* wave through inner core
J	*S* wave through inner core (designation only, wave not verified)
P'	Abbreviation for PKP
PP	Reflected *P* wave with two legs
PPP	Reflected *P* wave with three legs
SS	Reflected *S* wave with two legs
SP	*S* wave reflected as *P* wave
PS	*P* wave reflected as *S* wave
pP	*P*-wave with leg from focus to surface
sS	*S*-wave with leg from focus to surface
c	Wave reflected at outside boundary of outer core (e.g., *ScS*)
i	Wave reflected at outside boundary of inner core (e.g., *PKiKP*)
m	Number of reflections inside the outer boundary of outer core is $m-1$
d	Value in kilometers denoting the depth of a surface in the upper part of the Earth from which a seismic ray is reflected
h	Wave that may be reflected from a discontinuity around inner core
dif P, dif S	*P* or *S* waves that creep around the boundary between the mantle and outer core

Guide to Further Reading

Titles marked by an asterisk are more elementary treatments that are suitable for the general reader and undergraduate student.

Books that contain significant discussions on seismological explorations of the Earth's interior:

Aki, K., and P. G. Richards. *Quantitative Seismology: Theory and Methods,* Volumes I and II. San Francisco: W. H. Freeman and Company, 1980.

*Bolt, B. A. *Nuclear Explosions and Earthquakes: The Parted Veil.* San Francisco: W. H. Freeman and Company, 1976.

*Bolt, B. A. (Editor). *Earthquakes and Volcanoes, Readings from Scientific American.* San Francisco: W. H. Freeman and Company, 1980.

Bott, M. A. P. *The Interior of the Earth.* New York: St. Martin's Press, 1971.

Bullen, K. E. *An Introduction to the Theory of Seismology.* Cambridge, England: Cambridge University Press, 1963.

*Bullen, K. E. *The Interior of the Earth.* Chapter 27 of *Adventures in Earth History* (ed. Preston Cloud). San Francisco: W. H. Freeman and Company, 1970.

Bullen, K. E. *The Earth's Density.* London: Chapman and Hall, 1975.

Clark, S. P. (Editor). *Handbook of Physical Constants,* Geological Society of America Memoir 97, 1966.

*Eiby, G. A. *Earthquakes.* Auckland: Heinemann Educational Books, 1980.

*Fisher, O. *Physics of the Earth's Crust,* 2nd ed. London: Macmillan, 1889.

Garland, G. D. *Introduction to Geophysics: Mantle, Core and Crust.* Philadelphia: W. B. Saunders, 1971.

Gutenberg, B. *Physics of the Earth's Interior.* New York: Academic Press, 1959.

*Hodgson, J. H. *Earthquakes and Earth Structure.* Englewood Cliffs, N.J.: Prentice-Hall, 1964.

Jacobs, J. A. *The Earth's Core*. London: Pergamon, 1976.

Jeffreys, H. *The Earth*, 6th ed. Cambridge, England: Cambridge University Press, 1976.

*Press, F., and R. Siever. *Earth*, 3rd ed. San Francisco: W. H. Freeman and Company, 1982.

*Richter, C. F. *Elementary Seismology*. San Francisco: W. H. Freeman and Company, 1958.

Stacey, F. *Physics of the Earth*, 2nd ed. London: Pergamon, 1978.

Thompson, W. (later Lord Kelvin), and P. G. Tait. *Treatise on Natural Philosophy*. Cambridge, England: Cambridge University Press, 1879.

Verhoogen, J., F. J. Turner, L. E. Weiss, C. Wahrhaftig, and W. S. Fyfe. *The Earth: An Introduction to Physical Geology*. New York: Holt, Rinehart and Winston, 1970.

Review articles and selected papers that report work described in the text:

Alterman, Z., H. Jarosch, and C. L. Pekeris. "Oscillations of the Earth." *Proc. Roy. Soc. Lond. A 252*, 80–95, 1959.

*Anderson, D. L. "Seismology on Mars." *Earthquake Information Bulletin 11*, 120–126, 1979.

Backus, G., and F. Gilbert. "Uniqueness in the Inversion of Inaccurate Gross Earth Data." *Philos. Trans. Roy. Soc. Lond. A 266*, 123–192, 1970.

Birch, F. "Composition of the Earth's Mantle." *Geophys. J. Roy. Astro. Soc. 4*, 295–311, 1961.

*Bolt, B. A. "The Density Distribution Near the Base of the Mantle and Near the Earth's Center." *Phys. Earth and Planet, Interiors 5*, 301–311, 1972.

*Bolt, B. A. "The Fine Structure of the Earth's Interior." *Scientific American 228*, 24–33, March 1973 (offprint 906).

Bolt, B. A. "The Detection of *PKIIKP* and Damping in the Inner Core." *Annali di Geofisica 30*, 507–520, 1977.

Bolt, B. A. (Chairman). *U.S. Earthquake Observatories. Recommendations for a New National Network*, Panel Report, Committee on Seismology, National Academy Press, 1981.

Bolt, B. A., and D. R. Brillinger. "Estimation of Uncertainties in Eigenspectral Estimates from Decaying Geophysical Time Series." *Geophys. J. Roy. Astro. Soc. 59*, 593–603, 1979.

*Bolt, B. A., and J. S. Derr. "Free Bodily Vibrations of the Terrestrial Planets," *Vistas in Astronomy 11*, 69–102, 1969.

Bolt, B. A., and R. A. Uhrhammer. "Resolution Techniques for Density and Heterogeneity in the Earth." *Geophys. J. Roy. Astro. Soc. 42*, 419–435, 1975.

Branson, J. C., F. J. Moss, and F. J. Taylor. "Deep Crustal Reflection Seismic Test Survey, Mildura, Victoria and Broken Hill, N.S.W." *Bureau of Mineral Resources, Australia, Report 183*, 1976.

Bullen, K. E., and R. A. W. Haddon. "Some Recent Work on Earth Models with Special Reference to Core Structure." *Geophys. J. Roy. Astro. Soc. 34*, 31–38, 1973.

*Bush, S. G. "Discovery of the Earth's Core." *Am. J. Phys. 48*, 705–724, 1980.

Cleary, J. R. "The *S* Velocity of the Core-Mantle Boundary from Observations of Diffracted *S*." *Bull. Seism. Soc. Am. 59*, 1399–1405, 1969.

Cleary, J. R., and R. S. Anderssen. "Seismology and the Internal Structure of the Earth." In *The Earth, Its Origin, Structure and Evolution,* New York, Academic Press, 1979.

Doornbos, D. J., and J. C. Mondt. "*P* and *S* Waves Diffracted Around the Core and the Velocity Structure at the Base of the Mantle." *Geophys. J. Roy. Astro. Soc. 57,* 381–395, 1979.

Drake, L., and B. A. Bolt. "Love Waves Normally Incident at a Continental Boundary." *Bull. Seism. Soc. Am. 70,* 1103–1123, 1980.

Dziewonski, A. M., and D. L. Anderson. "Preliminary Reference Earth Model." *Physics of the Earth and Planetary Interiors 25,* 297–356, 1981.

Engdahl, E. R., E. H. Flinn, and C. Romney. "Seismic Waves Reflected from the Earth's Inner Core." *Nature 228,* 852–853, 1970.

Engdahl, E. R., and C. H. Schulz. "A Double Benioff Zone Beneath the Aleutians: An Unbending of the Lithosphere." *Geophys. Res. Letters 4,* 473–476, 1977.

Fukao, Y., K. Kanjo, and I. Nakamura. "Deep Seismic Zone as an Upper Mantle Reflector of Body Waves." *Nature 272,* 606–608 1978.

Haddon, R. A. W., and J. R. Cleary. "Evidence for Scattering of Seismic *PKP* Waves Near the Mantle-Core Boundary." *Phys. Earth and Planet. Interiors 8,* 211–234, 1974.

Hart, R. S., D. L. Anderson, and H. Kanamori. "The Effect of Attenuation on Gross Earth Models." *J. Geophys. Res. 82,* 1647, 1977.

Hasegawa, A., N. Umino, and A. Takagi. "Double-Planed Deep Seismic Zone and Upper-Mantle Structure in the Northeastern Japan Arc." *Geophys. J. Roy. Astro. Soc. 54,* 281–296, 1978.

Johnson, L. R. "Array Measurements of *P* Velocities in the Upper Mantle." *J. Geophys. Res. 70,* 6309–6325, 1967.

*Jordan, J. H. "The Deep Structure of the Continents." *Scientific American 240,* 92–107, January 1979 (offprint 935).

Jordan, J. H. "Structural Geology of the Earth's Interior." *Proc. Natl. Acad. Sci. U.S.A. 76,* 4192–4200, 1979.

Jordan, J. H., and D. L. Anderson. "Earth Structure from Free Oscillations and Travel-Times." *Geophys. J. Roy. Astro. Soc. 36,* 411–459, 1974.

Linde, A. T., and I. S. Sacks. "On Double Benioff Zones in Subduction Regions." Carnegie Institute of Washington *Year Book 78,* 517–520, 1978.

*Oldham, R. D. "On the Propagation of Earthquake Motion to Great Distances." *Philos. Trans. Roy. Soc. Lond. 194,* 135–174, 1900.

*Oliver, J. "Exploration of the Continental Basement by Seismic Reflection Profiling." *Nature 275,* 485–488, 1978.

Oliver, J. "Exploring the Basement of the North American Continent." *American Scientist 68,* 676–683, 1980.

*Press, F. "Resonant Vibrations of the Earth," *Scientific American 213,* 28–37, November 1965.

Smith, S. W. "An Investigation of the Earth's Free Oscillations." Ph.D. thesis, California Institute of Technology, 1961.

Smithson, S. B., J. Brewer, S. Kaufman, J. Oliver, and C. Hurich. "Nature of the Wind River Thrust, Wyoming, from COCORP Deep-Reflection Data and from Gravity Data." *Geology 6,* 648–652, 1978.

Stewart, I. C. F., and C. E. Keen. "Anomalous Upper Mantle Structure Beneath the Cretaceous Fogo Seamounts Indicated by *P*-Wave Reflection Delays." *Nature, 274* 788–791, 1978.

Stifler, J., and B. A. Bolt. "Eigenvibrations of a Non-Radially Symmetric Earth," *Geophys. J. Roy. Astro. Soc. 64,* 201–221, 1981.

*Taylor, S. R. "Structure and Evolution of the Moon." *Nature 281,* 105–110, 1979.

Verhoogen, J. "Energetics of the Earth." National Academy of Sciences, Washington, D.C., 1980.

Index